1992

Rebirth *of* Value

Rebirth *of* Value

Meditations on Beauty, Ecology, Religion, and Education

FREDERICK TURNER

STATE UNIVERSITY OF NEW YORK PRESS

Published by
State University of New York Press, Albany

© 1991   State University of New York

For information, address State University of New York
Press, State University Plaza, Albany, N.Y. 12246

Library of Congress Cataloging-in-Publication Data

Turner, Frederick, 1943–
   Rebirth of value : meditations on beauty, ecology, religion, and
education / Frederick Turner.
      p.   cm.
   Includes bibliographical references (p.   ).
   ISBN 0-7914-0473-0 (alk. paper). — ISBN 0-7914-0474-9 (pbk. :
alk. paper)
   1. Postmodernism.   2. Aesthetics, Modern—20th century.
3. Postmodernism—Religious aspects.   4. Education—Philosophy.
5. Ecology—Philosophy.   I. Title.
B831.2.T87   1991
146'.7—dc20   90-32500
                                                            CIP

10 9 8 7 6 5 4 3 2 1

146.7
T924

CONTENTS

144,648

ACKNOWLEDGMENTS

My thanks are due to the following periodicals for offering a first home to earlier versions of several of these essays: *Harper's, Chronicles, Missouri Review, Performing Arts Journal, American Theatre, Stanford Literary Review,* and *Restoration and Management Notes.* All of the essays have been revised somewhat for inclusion in the present volume.

It would take too many pages to list all of the people whose ideas, criticisms, advice, discoveries, and creative artworks have gone into the making of this book. Let me single out in an almost arbitrary way the names of a few whose contribution seems to cry out for my thanks: my colleagues Robert Corrigan, Alex Argyros, Zsuzsanna and Istvan Ozsvath, Stan Rupert, Fred Curchack, and David Channell; my mother, the anthropologist Edith Turner, my brother, the physicist Robert Turner, my brother Rory Turner who advised me on historical reenactments, and of course my late father Victor W. Turner; Bill Jordan, whose contribution in the area of ecological restoration was enormous; Lynda and Michael Sexson, Harvey Wheeler, Lewis Lapham, Frederick Feirstein, Dick Allen, Dana Gioia, Wade Newman, Emily Grosholz, Adrian Malone, Sandra Bradley, Ingo Rentschler, Jerre Levy, Amy Clampitt, Ihab Hassan, Colwyn Trevarthen, J. T. Fraser, John Miles Foley, Robert Kellogg, Tom Scheff, Judith Weissman, Roy Wagner, Ralph Cohen, Elizabeth and Helen Forman, Richard Hoppe, Cliff and Kuniko Weber, Joyce Parr, Martin Garhart, Daniel Fleckles, Joanne Hoover, Burton Raffel, Richard Schechner, John Hirsch, Jim O'Quinn, Speer Morgan, Virgil Nemoianu, Peter Viereck, Bonnie Marranca, Pat Howell, Edwin Watkins, Alma Fenwick, Arthur Redding, Victor Peterson, David Newman, Gretchen Sween, Randy Newman, Rodger Sorenson, Gail Thomas, Donald and Louise Cowan, Robert Sardello, and William Burford. I would also like to thank my wife, Mei Lin, for her deep, scholarly, and sensitive readings of Homer, Aeschylus, Virginia Woolf, and all those other subjects in which she is the tutor of my taste and the guide of my civility.

INTRODUCTION: A REBIRTH OF VALUE

A new spirit has begun to emerge in the natural sciences. The Nobelist Roger Sperry claims that the dominant paradigm in the brain sciences has changed profoundly. The old deterministic models, in which higher brain functions such as knowledge, values, and intentions were only intelligible as the passive results of underlying biological or environmental causes, have collapsed under the weight of evidence. It now becomes clear that the human personal mind has a powerfully determinative effect of its own, and that the whole is not only greater than the sum of its parts but also partly responsible for what they do. There is a "top-down"—whole to part—causality as well as the familiar "bottom-up"—part to whole—causality. More exciting still, the *combination* of top-down and bottom-up causality constitutes a nonlinear feedback system that is essentially unpredictable, though self-organizing and highly ordered. Order, hierarchy of function, and the efficacy of values not only coexist with freedom, open-endedness, heterarchy, creativity, and flexibility; they are the necessary precondition for them.

In another development, the discovery of the endorphins and enkephalins, the human brain-reward system, has profoundly undermined psychological determinism, liberating the study of motivation from its reduction to blocked or sublimated libido. And sociobiology, which once looked as if it would merely replace older reductionisms with genetic reductionism, has now recognized the complexity and open-endedness of the gene-culture coevolution cycle: genes are now seen not just as the determinants but also as the results of cultural and individual choices.

The feedback theme is now becoming dominant across a wide range of sciences. Everywhere the nonlinear, reflexive, iterative, self-organizing, dissipative, period-doubling, turbulent, open-ended, or fractal systems that are associated with feedback have appeared at the heart of nature's mysteries.

Such systems are often called chaotic, but "chaotic" in this sense really means more deeply ordered than meets the eye. Not that we must abandon our old linear calculus and our sophisticated Fourier analysis of regularities and repetitions: beyond the feedbacks *within* turbulence, there is a still more remarkable feedback *between* turbulence and smooth, linear, or periodic flow. The universe is not merely unpredictable: it is a partly predictable interplay between the predictable and the unpredictable. Indeed, if it were not so, there would be no adaptive use for memory: for if the universe were totally unpredictable, a knowledge of its past would be useless for the future; but if it were completely predictable, an organism would be much better off with a set of automatic reflexes than with a memory. In other words, not only are the higher organisms free and self-determining, so is the universe itself; and this, on reflection now, is only commonsense, for if either were unfree, the organism would not survive.

Together with chaos science has come a reinterpretation of quantum theory. The revelation of quantum theory now appears not so much that the fundamental level of physical existence is chaotic in the old sense—indefinable, uncertain, unordered—as that chaos has its own way of collapsing into order, definiteness, and certainty. Not that this "decision" produces a dead state of rigidity and stasis: on the contrary. It immediately opens up new realms of potentiality, on higher and more complex levels than the old. Thus, when the universe during the Big Bang cooled sufficiently to allow probabilistic subatomic particles to combine and collapse into relatively stable atoms and molecules, an entirely new world of freedom— chemical recombination—was opened up, with far more permutations that were possible in the hot and transient soup of quantum particles. (On the level of literary critical theory this insight would correspond to a rejection of any naive deconstruction that reduced a text to a hot soup of traces, of "differances," to use Derrida's wordplay: what is of far more significance is that those differances collapse together into meanings that make possible further meanings and further meanings still, in an evolutionary ecology of meaning which does not merely erase but subsumes its predecessors.)

A new environmental science has begun to suggest a new environmental ethics. At its center is the Gaia Hypothesis, which unifies plate tectonics, macrogeochemistry (the study of such global phenomena as the carbon and nitrogen cycles, ice ages, and the greenhouse effect), the new bacteriology of Margulis, Sonea, and Panisset, traditional ecology, and ecological restoration theory. In this view the planet is a single self-regulating (and self-improving, and perhaps eventually self-reproducing!) organism in which we human beings have an important part to play. If we follow up the implications of the theory, even our genetic engineering is but a faster and more directed version of the recombinant DNA exchange that has been going on since the beginning of life itself, through the transfer between bacteria of small replicons such as plasmids and viruses, or by sexual reproduction. The old environmentalism, with its traces of a romantic weariness with humanity and its comfortable absolutism of belief, cannot survive this new perspective. The essays in the second major section of this book, on postmodern ecological ethics, explore these perspectives in detail.

Evolution reappears in this new synthesis as the central paradigm of all knowledge. In the nineteenth century, when Darwin first proposed its elegant mechanism, evolution was taken to imply the exact opposite of what it actually implies. Two ideas, the physical determinism of Newton and Laplace, and the historical determinism of Hegel and Comte, so dominated the European imagination that *any* idea, even one like evolution which radically and totally *refutes* determinism, would have been taken and twisted into a confirmation of it. Remarkably, even the opponents of evolution automatically bought the proposition that it must, because it was scientific, be reductionist and determinist. Instead, evolution should have been taken as a reasoned proof that the universe could produce radical novelty and unpredictable synthesis without any violation of natural laws, and thus that freedom, creativity, and transcendence are not only permissible in the universe, but part of its essential dynamic. This more accurate view of evolution is now gradually coming into focus, though alas it is often paradoxically opposed by the very people—religious, artistic, and humanistic—for whom it offers the greatest intellectual rewards.

David Griffin points out perceptively that the deterministic and reductionistic view of the physical universe was originally encouraged by theistic Christians in order to mandate a place for a transcendent God in the production of creativity and freedom, but when the "dead" machine of the universe turned out to be quite capable of getting along without supernatural help, they were hoist by their own petard. The new scientific view of the universe is that it is a *living* machine: an organic mechanism which generates and is nurtured by freedom, creativity, and self-transcendence—and which may, as we do, have a wholeness that is greater than the sum of its parts, a Soul which has been the inner goal of all religions. If this is so, we—all the higher intelligences of the universe, whatever and wherever we are—are the nervous system of God's world-body.

Evolution now appears to be central not only to the content and form of knowledge, but also to its growth and development. A new evoutionary epistemology and dialectic of discourse seems to be coming into focus. Between single absolutist hegemonic worldviews, which generate a certainty of truth at the expense of its richness and variety, and relativist and pluralist worldviews, whose claim to certainty is so diffident that it enfeebles and thus corrupts and trivializes the mind that entertains them, we see appear an evolving ecology of worldviews, competing or cooperating, but always tending toward the production of more comprehensive and also more sensitive and thus concrete ideas. This evolutionary drama or story is both unified and plural: like species that conquer an ecological niche, the most vital ideas subdue, co-opt, or cooperate with their competitors only to branch out and radiate into new niches. Nor is this as ruthless a process as might be implied by the language: slavery and racism are examples of ideas which rightly succumbed to their competition.

The new cybernetic technology, together with the cognitive science of which it is the inspiration and instrument, is the beginning of a deeper innervation of the physical world, so that the relatively numb tissue of the material levels of physicality may be given a tongue and a language, and connected by neural/ cybernetic interfaces to the quick imaginative intelligence of human beings. Many religious and philosophical traditions so yearn for an inspirited universe that they have been unwilling to accept the actual slow stupidity of most of nature, its deadly conformity, its slavery to habit, its hidebound repetitiveness much of the time. Only in favored environments, like that of the Earth, has nature had the resources —the steep gradient of available energy—to follow its wildest and sweetest promptings and give birth to the freer forms of sentient existence. But perhaps one day we will be able to transform kinds of matter other than our own into entities that can speak and feel and know themselves and join in the higher conversation of world history. So, paradoxically again, the very technology that some religious people find so threatening may help bring about that animate and spirited universe after which they hanker.

We will increasingly see in political philosophy and critical theory a recovery of the idea of hierarchy as a central concept, but shorn of its old association with rigidity. The kind of hierarchy postulated by the most recent theories of neural organization, physical and ecological feedback systems, evolution, and artificial intelligence is dynamic, open-ended, and "tangled" in its higher reaches, as Hofstadter puts it, with heterarchical complications. The hierarchy of temporalities, by which such philosophers as J. T. Fraser propose to replace earlier incoherent theories of time as an absolute dimension, is likewise tangled by the inclusion within higher temporalities of the lower ones out of which they evolved, together with the characteristic conflicts between and within temporal levels.

In anthropology and sociology we shall see dramatistic models of social process arising wherein, instead of the old alternatives of absolute social truth or relativistic pluralism, we will see society as a loosely unified drama of different viewpoints evolving through mutual feedback toward a more reflexive and comprehensive, but also more fully embodied awareness. These ideas are pursued in the final section of this book, on postmodern education.

Many of the scientific developments sketched in this book are already beginning to reflect themselves in the arts. In a sense this appropriation by the arts is the repayment of a debt, for art was until the advent of modernism the arena of our deepest thought about reflexive self-ordering feedback systems and the beautiful fractal morphology they display. As I have argued in an earlier book, *Natural Classicism,* the ancient forms, genres, and traditions of the arts, which are culturally universal and tuned to the human nervous system, derive from and help to continue the deep feedback loop between human biology and human culture, as well as making us aware of the relationship itself and thus able to direct it to some degree. The fate of modernist esthetic theory is in some ways the obverse of modernist philosophy of science. Whereas our error in thinking about science was to imagine a world of rigid deterministic order, our error in thinking about art was to imagine an art that was totally random, meaningless, and disordered. In neither conception do we find true freedom. A

constructive postmodernism would instead recognize the autonomy and self-organizing creativity of both nature and art, and
see their deep kinship as indeed a continuity. Performance,
then, would emerge as the equivalent in art to that collapse of
the wave function into actuality which occurs in nature when
an observer compels a probabilistic system to declare itself
unambiguously and thus to take part in the continued evolution of the universe. These ideas are further explored in the
first section of this book, on the new esthetics.

Clearly these developments also have the profoundest implications for religion. Science now shows us a universe that has
no need of an *external* divine drama to give it meaning and
value: in itself the actual history of the universe, as it comes
into focus before our eyes, is more beautiful, more morally
significant, and more humanly relevant than any of the fabu-
lous approximations to it that traditional theologies and
theogonies have devised. The divine drama is here right now;
we, and the rest of the universe, are living it out. Not that the
old religions were wrong; they were as right as they could be
without a detailed look at the world-body of the gods. Science
more than confirms their guesses. Instead of eternity we have
a dynamic future whose mysterious wholenesses, as final
causes, call into being our best creative actions. The essays in
the section on religion take up some of the issues raised by this
way of thinking.

The new perspective clearly presents an enormous challenge
to the academy; the final section of this book, on education,
attempts to face that challenge. What is demanded is no less
than a complete transformation of the disciplinary departmental structure of our universities to reflect the unity and
hierarchical/heterarchical structure of the universe itself and
of any viable knowledge of it; and a profound revision of the
essentially deterministic and power-based assumptions of the
social and human sciences. Together with these changes must
come a new, more personal, more humane, and more performative pedagogy. Knowledge is not something that can be stored
or accumulatd or simply transmitted en bloc. It exists only as
it lives, as it is shared, as it acts, and as it is used. It is like
love, which is not possessed but given, less a noun than a
verb. And yet every action disambiguates knowledge, even as
it opens up the world as a richer and more reflexive set of
potentials. We cannot remain content with the ambiguity of
our knowledge; we must risk it and give it away by forcing it
to act and disambiguate itself on the stage of the world.

Out of these developments will come, I believe a new spirit in society. There will be a gradual moderation of the wave of hatred that has swept the world since the French Revolution. We will be less paranoid about science and technology, as those fields become based less on inanimate mechanistic paradigms and adapted more to the richness and subtlety of human understanding. There will be a relaxation of the hostility between the world of business and production on the one hand, and the intellectuals, academics, and artists of our Brahmin caste on the other. We will find ways to integrate our most courageous, active, and creative powers into the harmonious evolution of the ecology: nature is not so different from us, and its reflexive feedbacks are but an earlier and slower form of our self-awareness. We need no longer see ourselves as guilty by virtue of our self-consciousness, and as alienated from a natural world of innocence. Nature is no more innocent than we are, and self-knowledge is not the obstacle but the driving force of universal creativity. When we are more at peace with nature we will be able to recover the natural values which we now regard with such suspicion, regenerated on a new scientific and artistic basis.

The essays in this collection were composed for different audiences, within the languages of different communities of expertise, and with somewhat different cognitive and artistic goals. But to have homogenized them for the purposes of this book would, I believe, have been a mistake. Thus the book has been edited only to remove some of the more obvious redundancies. Moreover, it is not intended to be a work of scholarship, but rather an arena of ideas and a stimulus to new perspectives. Perhaps it can best recommend itself as a large-scale assessment of our culture and our times from the point of view of a poet, and one of the only assessments of such scope that exist in this age of specialization.

Although it draws on the author's scholarly research in a number of fields, such as biological foundations of esthetics, literary studies, the history and philosophy of science and technology, the history of gardening and ecological thought, performance studies, the oral tradition, cultural anthropology, and brain science, this book is not designed as an exhaustive proof of its suggestions. Nor is it simply a popularization. Instead, it seeks to restore an old and lost genre, the creative general essay. The book claims no affiliation with any current body of political opinion or academic orthodoxy and will, I believe, be most useful to those who do not attempt to fit it into the intellectual framework of some existing school of thought, such as poststructuralism, neoconservatism, neomarxism, environmentalism, process theology, or the like. For readers who wish to explore its ideas further there is a list of readings at the end of the book; but for some of its suggestions they will, I hope, find no outside authority.

A NEW ESTHETICS

This section begins with an essay that develops a new esthetic theory based on the coevolution of the biological and cultural elements of the human nervous system. The essay goes on to a broader redefinition of beauty as embedded in the fundamental generative processes of the universe—and thus possessing a real, not just a subjective, existence. Recent developments in the theory of chaos, nonlinear processes, and self-organizing systems point the way.

A second essay describes the historical processes that led to the widespread destructiveness and anomie of late modernist art. They include the misinterpretation of nineteenth-century scientistic ideas of determinism, the metaphor of combustion in our technological and industrial methods of production, the demographics of the massive increase in world population, and the reductionistic psychology of the realist novel. Alternative directions, which have recently opened up, are described.

In a third essay recent productions of Shakespeare's The Tempest *are analyzed, demonstrating the postmodern themes of eclecticism, neoclassicism, reflexivity, magic realism, and the rebirth of philosophical art.*

I   On Beauty

What is beauty? The very concept is rejected by many contemporary artists and estheticians.

Part of our predicament is that the arts have been cut off from the sciences; cut off, that is, from any coherent and well-founded and *surprising* conception of the cosmos that we live in and of our own bodies and nervous systems. Thus a scientific answer to the question of beauty has been until recently unavailable to artists and estheticians. At the same time science itself has been until recently—though there are encouraging signs of change—fragmented, disunified, and mortally afraid of value questions. In practice all true scientists prefer beautiful scientific theories to ugly ones. But this aspect of science is a long way from the routine of institutionalized science and has seldom penetrated through to the arts.

Robert Pirsig put the matter thus:

> At present we're snowed under with an irrational expansion of blind data-gathering in the sciences, because there's no rational format for any understanding of scientific creativity. At present we're also snowed under with a lot of stylishness in the arts—thin art—because there's very little assimilation or extension into underlying form. We have artists with no scientific knowledge and scientists with no artistic knowledge and both with no spiritual sense of gravity at all. And the result is not just bad, it's ghastly. (*Zen and the Art of Motorcycle Maintenance,* p. 287)

That "spiritual sense of gravity" is close to what I mean by beauty; but to give this phrase some meaning we must pursue our first question without qualms that analysis will destroy it. Analysis could only destroy it if it had no concrete existence—which is what its critics claim, that beauty is an illusion in the

3

eye of the beholder, an eye preconditioned by social convention and economic interest. What this essay will do is argue
that beauty is an objective reality.

If not beauty, what do contemporary artists propose to
themselves as the meaning of their work? There are three
usual answers to this question. The first is that it is enough to
be new, disturbing, analytically interesting. If there is no
further depth in a work of art, does not this boil down, hon-
estly, to being what Pirsig calls stylish?—fashionable? Is not
such art merely a sort of demonstration of critical ideas? The
second approach is to be personal. In this view the work of art
has a quality derived from the mysterious and intangible
nature of the individual. But does not this answer simply shift
the problem from what makes an engaging work of art to what
makes an engaging human being?—all the self-expression in
the world cannot make interesting a personality we do not like;
indeed, quite the reverse. The third answer is that art should
be socially, economically, and politically correct. There are
many variations of this: Marxist art; the simulation of regional
or vernacular art; the art of gender politics; functionalist art.
But again the question is begged: if we cannot recognize a
good work of art, how can we recognize a good society or
economy or polity? Can art be subordinate to politics, and still
be distinguished from propaganda? Why should not art be the
free and vital source of political ideas, rather than their servant
and vehicle? And is not functionalism merely a permit for art
to be guided by unguided technology? These issues have been
gone over in weary detail by much contemporary critical and
esthetic theory; there is no need to dwell on them here, where
much more exciting possibilities await us.

Let us return to the idea of beauty as the goal and meaning
of art. But what is beauty in the most general sense? What
nontrivial description could hold true for a beautiful Inuit
mask, a beautiful man or woman, the laws of thermodynamics,
an Arcadian landscape, a picture of an Arcadian landscape, a
Bach canon, the Mandelbrot set (with its microcosmic corona
of Julia sets), a flowering chestnut tree, the theory of evolution
by natural selection, an African ritual dance, and Yeats's
"Byzantium"?

All human societies possess the concept of beauty, often
with a very precise vocabulary and a tradition of argument
about it. People see (hear, touch, taste, smell) the beautiful, and
recognize it by a natural intuition and a natural pleasure.

Even animals do: antiphonal birdsong, the brilliant shapes and colors of flowers (what more precise record could there be of the esthetic preferences of bees?), and the gorgeous ritual mating garments of tropical fishes and birds of paradise, all attest to a more than utilitarian attraction in certain forms of organization.

This "natural intuition" is for us human beings activated, sensitized, and deepened by culture; that is, a natural capacity of the nervous system now incorporates a cultural feedback loop, and also uses the physical world, through art and science, as part of its own hardware. The theory of such a training or sensitization, the incorporation of this cultural feedback loop, the plugging of it into the prepared places in our brains, is what I call "natural classicism." In a previous book by that title much of the evidence for the following ideas is cited; the task here is not to prove its contentions, but to explore its further implications.

The foundation of the natural classical perspective is that the universe, and we, evolved. This fact entails two truths about beauty: a special evolutionary truth and a general evolutionary truth.

The special evolutionary truth is that our capacity to perceive and create beauty is a characteristic of an animal that evolved. Beauty is thus in some way a biological adaptation and a physiological reality: the experience of beauty can be connected to the activity of actual neurotransmitters in the brain, endorphins and enkephalins. When we become addicted to a drug such as heroin or cocaine we do so because their molecular structure resembles that of the chemistries of joy that the brain feeds to itself.

What is the function of pleasure from an evolutionary point of view? The pleasure of eating is clearly a reward for the labor of getting ourselves something to eat. Certainly few would go to the extraordinary metabolic expense and aggravation of finding a willing member of the opposite sex and reproducing with him or her unless there were a very powerful inducement to do so. We are presented with this very great pleasure of beauty, for which artists will starve in garrets and for whose mimicked substitutes rats and addicts will happily neglect food and sex. What is it a reward for? What adaptive function does it serve, that is so much more important than immediate nourishment and even the immediate opportunity to reproduce the species?

Freud claimed that the esthetic was merely a sublimated form of libido. But the new knowledge about neurotransmitters and brain reward renders this theory invalid. Beauty, it seems, has a perfectly adequate chemistry of its own, without having to borrow a bit of the pleasure-chemistry of sex. We must reexamine the whole relationship between the beauty that men and women find in each other and sexual desire. Could it not be that the truth is exactly opposite to what Freud thought?— that much of what we think of as sex is actually a relaxed or dissipated form of esthetic excitement; that sexual attraction is not enough by itself to assure the reproductive pair-bond, and that it must borrow—or sublimate!—part of the energy of spiritual experience! What might a psychoanalysis based on such ideas look like?

Let us return to the question: what is the beauty-experience a reward for? To answer this question we need to know a little about the timing of human evolution, as it is becoming clear from the work of paleoanthropologists, paleolinguists, archaeologists, and paleogeneticists. The crucial point is that there is a peculiar overlap between the last phases of human biological evolution and the beginnings of human cultural evolution, an overlap of one to five million years, depending on how the terms are defined. In any case, there was a long period during which human culture could exert a powerful, indeed dominant, selective pressure upon the genetic material of the species and thus upon the final form it has taken (if ours is the final form).

For over a million years the major genetic determinant in the environment of our genus was our own culture. A creature that is living under cultural constraints is a creature that is undergoing an intensive process of domestication. Consider wheat, dogs, apple trees, pigeons: how swiftly and how dramatically they have been changed by human selective breeding! But we domesticated ourselves. There is a limestone cave near Zhoukoudian in northern China where human beings lived almost continuously for close to a quarter of a million years. It is filled almost to the roof with eighteen feet of compacted human debris—ash, bedplaces, bones. At the bottom, the oldest layers contain great hamhanded hammerstones, cutting clubs with a shard knocked off for a blade, and the clumsy bones and skulls of Homo erectus. At the top, there are delicate leafshaped flint arrowheads, fine awls and augers, featherlike knives; and human jawbones made elegant by cookery, braincases made ample and capacious by ritual.

Imagine—and we hardly need to imagine this, for we have so many examples in our experience, if we could only see them as examples—imagine a mating ritual, which directly affects the reproductive success of the individuals within a species. Those who are neurologically capable and adept at the complex nuances of the ritual would have a much better chance of getting a mate and leaving offspring. Now imagine that this ritual is being handed down from generation to generation not just by genetic inheritance, but also, increasingly, by cultural transmission: imitation, instruction, and eventually language (did it evolve in order to facilitate this transmission?).

If a behavior is handed down purely by genetic inheritance, any variations on it which result from individual differences and special environmental and social circumstances will be wiped out by the death of the individuals of a given generation and will not be transmitted to their offspring. Of course if over thousands of years those individual differences lead to improved rates of survival, and if those special circumstances persist, then there may be a selective advantage in the behavior as modified by the variation, and that variation will become frozen into the genes. But this is a very slow process: the learning is being done at the genetic level, not at the social or mental level.

But in the thought-experiment that we have commenced, changes in the ritual can be handed down very quickly, in only one generation; and so the faster system of transmission will tend to drive and direct the slower system of transmission. That is, cultural modifications in the ritual will tend to confer a decisive selective advantage upon those members of the species that are genetically endowed with greater neural complexity, a superior capacity for learning the inner principles of the ritual which remain the same when its surface changes, for following and extending the ritual's subtleties, and for recognizing and embodying the values that the ritual creates. Cultural evolution will drive biological evolution. This species, of course, is ourselves: perhaps what created us as human beings was an improved lovesong. In the beginning, indeed, was the word.

In this scenario the idea of beauty clearly has a central place. The capacity for recognizing and creating beauty is a competence that we possess, a competence that was selected for by biocultural coevolution: it is both a power that the "mating ritual" of human and prehuman culture demanded and sharpened, and a value generated by that ritual that it was in our reproductive interest to be able to recognize and embody. Such an analysis might well adjust the balance of traditional paleoanthropology, which has been perhaps excessively concerned with with hairy males with flint axes, and begin to provide, if not a feminist anthropology, then a human one. To be, and to be able to recognize, a beautiful human being, and to desire to mix one's seed with his or hers, might be a survival strategy that drove the flowering of Homo sapiens. Already some of our examples of beauty—the man and woman, the Inuit mask, the African dance at least, and perhaps several of the others—might begin to fit together under a reasonably rich description.

What are the results of this coevolution in the neurobiology of esthetic experience? Simply to be able to ask this question— that it should be reasonable, indeed predicted by a solid theory, for beauty to have a pancultural neurobiological base—overturns modernist and most postmodernist esthetics. The evolutionary perspective suggests that we have inherited a number of related natural-classical genres or systems by which we generate, recognize, and appreciate beauty. What are these genres?

The experimental neuropsychologist Ernst Pöppel and I have investigated one of them in some detail—poetic meter, or what we have called the neural lyre. All over the world human beings compose and recite poetry in poetic meter; all over the world the meter has a line-length of about three seconds, tuned to the three-second acoustic information-processing pulse in the human brain. Our acoustic present is three seconds long— we remember echoically and completely three seconds' worth of acoustic information, before it is passed on to a longer-term memory system, where it is drastically edited, organized for significant content, and pushed down to a less immediate level of consciousness.

If a natural brain rhythm, like the ten cycle per second alpha rhythm—or the three second audial present—is "driven" or amplified by an external rhythmic stimulus, the result can be large changes in brain state and brain chemistry, and consequently in the amount and kind of information that the brain can absorb, and in the kind of higher-level processing it can put to work.

We showed that in addition to these effects, poetic meter contained within the line a regular pulse of syllable-patterns,

made of heavy and light, long or short, tone-changing or
unchanging, against which significant and expressive variations could be played. For instance, the English iambic pattern
consists of a regular pulse of one unstressed and one stressed
syllable, thus: -/ . But consider this stanza from Yeats's
"Byzantium," which is based on the same iambic (-/) pattern
of syllables, yet varies freely on it without losing touch with it:

> / - - / - / - / - -
> *Miracle, bird, or human handiwork,*
> / / - - - / - / - -
> *More miracle than bird or handiwork,*
> / - - - / - / - /
> *Planted on the starlit golden bough,*
> / - - / - / - /
> *Can like the cocks of Hades crow,*
> / - - / - / - / - /
> *Or, by the moon embittered, scorn aloud*
> - / - - / - / -
> *In glory of changeless metal*
> / - / - / -
> *Common bird or petal*
> - / - / - - - / - /
> *And all complexities of mire or blood.*

The difference between the expected rhythm and the actual
rhythm carries information, as a tune does, or as a line does in
a drawing; and that information is processed and understood
not with the linguistic left brain, but with the musical and
spatial right brain. Thus, unlike ordinary language, poetic
language comes to us in a "stereo" neural mode, so to speak,
and is capable of conveying feelings and ideas that are usually
labeled nonverbal; the genre itself is a biocultural feedback
loop that makes us able to use much more of our brain than we
normally can.

We need not go into this kind of detail with the other genres,
but they show the same kind of fascinating interplay between
inherited biological and learned cultural factors. Let us just list
a few of them.

1. The metrical "operator" of music, which is related to
   but different from the poetic metrical operator, and
   which also connects with dance. It is very highly
   developed in African drum rhythms.

2. The reflexive or dramatic operator, by which we are able to simulate other people's consciousness and point of view in imaginative models (containing miniature models of the other person's model of us, and so on), and set them into coherent theatrical interaction. "O wad some pow'r the giftie gie us," says Robert Burns, "To see oursels as others see us!" This natural-classical genre does exactly that.

3. The narrative operator, that genre by which we give time a complex tense-structure, full of might-have-beens and should-be's, conditionals, subjunctives, branches, hopes, and memories. Fundamentally the narrative operation constructs a series of events which have the curious property of being retrodictable (each one seems inevitable once it has happened) but not predictable (before it happens, we have no sound basis on which to foretell it); which is why we want to know what happens next. This operator comes with a large collection of archetypal myths and stories, such as the Swan Princess, which are fundamentally identical all over the world, because their seeds are in our genes.

4. The color-combination preferences that are associated with the so-called color wheel.

5. A similar visual detail-frequency preference system, which makes us prefer pictures and scenes with a complexly balanced hierarchy of high-frequency information (dense textures and small details) ranging through to low-frequency information (large general shapes and compositions). Consider, for instance, Japanese prints, or the Arcadian landscape paintings of Poussin and Claude.

6. A representational operator (unique to human beings), whereby we can reverse the process of visual perception and use our motor system to represent what we see by drawing, painting, or sculpting.

7. Musical tonality and the inexhaustible language it opens up, from Chinese classical music, through Balinese gamelan, to the fugues and canons of Bach.

And many more. Researchers of great boldness and brilliance are working to clarify the neuropsychology and anthropology of these systems; their results so far are described in a recent book entitled *Beauty and the Brain.*

As yet this list is just a list, with no systematic classification and no attempt to organize its members according to criteria of greater or lesser neural generality. But it does indicate that the forms of the arts are not arbitrary, but are rooted in our biological inheritance. To say this is not to imply that the natural-classical genres are constraints, or limits upon the expressive powers of the arts. Quite the reverse; they are like what computer enthusiasts call turbos—programs or hardware that can accelerate and improve the operation of a computer. These systems, which incorporate a cultural feedback loop into the brain's processing, can enormously deepen and broaden its powers. Language itself may be one of the most comprehensive and earliest of them. They are not constraints any more than the possession of a hammer or a screwdriver is a constraint upon our carpentry; but their use must be learned. An esthetic education that assumes that genres are obstacles to creativity, and which thus does not bother to teach them, deprives our children of their inheritance.

So much for the special evolutionary truth about beauty. Without the general evolutionary truth, it would be meaningful only in a practical sense, it would leave out that tremble of philosophical insight that we associate with beauty, and would ignore the beauty that we find in nature and in the laws of science. It is not enough, from an evolutionary point of view, that individuals within a species should be endowed with a species-specific sense of beauty related to cooperation and sexual selection, even if the selection favors big brains, sensitivity, and artistic grace. The whole species must benefit from possessing a sense of beauty. This could only be the case if beauty is a real characteristic of the universe, one that it would be useful—adaptive—to know. How might this be?

What I want to suggest is that the experience of beauty is a recognition of the deepest tendency or theme of the universe as a whole. This may seem a very strange thing to say; but there is a gathering movement across many of the sciences that indicates that the universe does have a deep theme or tendency, a leitmotif which we can begin very tentatively to describe, if not fully understand.

Let us play with an idea of Kant's and see what we get if we treat the esthetic as something analogous to perception. Imagine dropping a rock on the floor. The rock reacts by bouncing and by making a noise, and perhaps undergoes some slight internal change; we would not imagine that it felt anything approaching a sensation.

Now imagine that you drop a worm on the floor; the impact might cause it to squirm, as well as merely to bounce and to produce a sound of impact. The worm, we would say, feels a sensation; but from the worm's point of view it is not a sensation of anything in particular; the worm does not construct, with its primitive nerve ganglia, anything as complex as an external world filled with objects like floors and experimenters.

Now imagine that you drop a guinea pig. Clearly it would react, as the rock does, and also feel sensations, as the worm does. But we would say in addition that it perceives the floor, the large, dangerous animal that has just released it, and the dark place under the table where it may be safe. Perception is as much beyond sensation as sensation is beyond mere physical reaction. Perception constructs a precise, individuated world of solid objects out there, endowed with color, shape, smell, and acoustic and tactile properties. It is generous to the outside world, giving it properties it did not necessarily possess until some advanced vertebrate was able, through its marvelously parsimonious cortical world-construction system, to provide them. Perception is both more global, more holistic, than sensation—because it takes into account an entire outside world—and more exact, more particular, because it recognizes individual objects and parts of objects.

Now if you were a dancer and the creature that you dropped were a human being, a yet more astonishing capacity comes into play. One could write a novel about how the dance partners experience this drop, this gesture. Whole detailed worlds of implication, of past and future, of interpretive frames, come into being; and the table and the dancing floor do not lose any of the guinea pig's reality, but instead take on richnesses, subtleties, significant details, held as they are within a context both vaster and more clearly understood. What is this awareness, that is to perception what perception is to sensation, and sensation to reaction? The answer is: esthetic experience. Esthetic experience is as much more constructive, as much more generous to the outside world, as much more holistic, and as much more exact and particularizing than ordinary perception, as ordinary perception is than mere sensation. Thus by ratios we may ascend from the known to the very essence of the knower. Esthetic perception is not a vague and touchy-feely thing relative to ordinary perception; quite the reverse. This is why, given an infinite number of theories that will logically explain the facts, scientists will sensibly always choose the most beautiful theory. For good reason: this is the way the world works.

Beauty in this view is the highest integrative level of understanding and the most comprehensive capacity for effective action. It enables us to go with, rather than against, the deepest tendency or theme of the universe, to be able to model what will happen and adapt to or change it. Such benefits might well be worth the enormous metabolic expense of the brain, that organ that spends a third of the body's oxygen and sugar, and for which the body will willingly sacrifice itself.

But this line of investigation has clearly brought us to a question which it seems audacious to ask in this antimetaphysical age. Let us ask it anyway: what *is* the deepest tendency or theme of the universe?

Let us make another list, a list of descriptions or characteristics of that theme or tendency. We can always adjust or change the list if we want.

1. Unity in multiplicity—the universe does seem to be one, though it is full of an enormous variety and quantity of things. Our best knowledge about its beginning, if it had one, is that everything in the universe was contracted into a single hot dense atom; or if it had no beginning, then it is bounded by a single space-time continuum out of which all forms of matter and energy emerge.

2. Complexity within simplicity: the universe is very complicated, yet it was generated by very simple physical laws, like the laws of thermodynamics.

3. Generativeness and creativity: the universe generates a new moment every moment, and each moment has genuine novelties. Its tendency or theme is that it should not just stop. As it cooled, it produced all the laws of chemistry, all the new species of animals and plants, and finally ourselves and our history.

4. Rhythmicity: the universe can be described as a gigantic, self-nested scale of vibrations, from the highest-frequency particles, which oscillate with an energy

of ten million trillion giga-electron volts, to the slowest conceivable frequency (or deepest of all notes), which vibrates over a period sufficient for a single wave to cross the entire universe and return. Out of these vibrations, often in the most delicate and elaborate mixtures or harmonies of tone, everything is made.

5. Symmetry: shapes and forms are repeated or mirrored in all physical structures, whether at the subatomic, the atomic, the crystalline, the chemical, the biological, or the anthropological levels of reality. And the more complex and delicate the symmetry, the more opportunities it presents for symmetry-breaking, the readjustment of the system toward a new equilibrium, and thus adaptation toward even more comprehensive symmetries.

6. Hierarchical organization: big pieces of the universe contain smaller pieces, and smaller pieces contain smaller pieces still, and so on. Relatively big pieces, such as planets and stars, control to some extent—through their collective gravitational and electromagnetic fields—the behavior of the smaller pieces of which they are composed, while the smaller pieces together determine what the larger pieces are to begin with. We see the same hierarchical organization, much more marvelously complex and precise, in the relationship of the smallest parts of the human body to the highest levels of its organization, from elementary particles through atoms, molecules, cells, organelles, and organs, to the neural synthesis that delegates its control down the chain. Consider also the elegant hierarchy of support, control, cooperation, and dependency that one finds in the parts and whole of a Bach canon.

Of course this hierarchy is also complicated and "tangled," as Douglas Hofstadter puts it, by the mutual interference of entities at different levels of it, and by systemic transformations; an ecology, a food chain, is always changing, even if very slowly. But if such disruptions overwhelm the hierarchical frame, then the system as a whole has died, and its elements can then identify themselves only as a part of some other, perhaps cruder, hierarchical system. Thus the cells of my muscles when I am dead no longer obey my nervous system, but are either commandeered by the organization of worms and bacteria, or become part of the even more primitive systems of organic chemistry or physics.

7. Self-similarity: related to the hierarchical property is a marvelous property now being investigated by chaos theorists and fractal mathematicians: the smaller parts of the universe often resemble in shape and structure the larger parts of which they are components, and those larger parts in turn resemble the still larger systems that contain them. This property is in fact a kind of symmetry, but a symmetry not in different directions but on different scales. The scaling element makes an important difference, for the symmetry of form does not exist between two elements that are spatially separated from each other; one element is part of the fine structure of the other and can therefore interfere with it in a creative way. Thus the symmetry of self-similarity is a very rich field for the kind of symmetry-breaking which can generate new symmetries, new hierarchies, new beings.

Like Dante's *Divine Comedy,* in which the three-line stanza of its microcosm is echoed in the trinitarian theology of its middle-level organization and in the tripartite structure of the whole poem, so the universe tends to echo its themes at different scales, but with variations and interferences that give life to the whole. If you look at the branches of a tree (Yeats's chestnut tree, perhaps, that "great-rooted blossomer") you can see how the length of a twig stands in a similar—but not quite the same—relation to the length of the small branches as the small branches stand to the large branches, and the large branches to the trunk. You can find this pattern in all kinds of phenomena—electrical discharges, frost-flowers, the annual patterns of rise and decline in competing animal populations, stock market fluctuations, weather formations and clouds, the bronchi of the lungs, corals, turbulent waters, and so on. And this harmonious yet dynamic relation of small to large is *beautiful.*

Now these descriptions would be immediately recognized by scientists in many fields as belonging to feedback processes and the structures that are generated by them. Indeed, it is often difficult to tell the process apart from the product: how can we tell the dancer from the dance? *The fundamental tendency or theme of the universe, in short, is reflexivity or feedback.* We are beginning to understand more and more clearly that the universe is a phenomenon of turbulence, the result of a nested set of feedback processes. Hence, it is dynamic and open-ended: open-ended, moreover, precisely in and because of its continual attempt to come to closure, to fall to a stop. Moreover, as with any dynamic nonlinear open feedback process, the universe continually generates new frames and dimensions, new rules and constraints, and its future states are too complicated to be calculated by any conceivable computer made out of the universe as it is. It is retrodictable but not predictable, like a good—a beautiful—story.

In other words, the universe is what we call *free*. We human beings possess a larger degree of freedom, perhaps, than any of the other parts of the world, but we are not unique in being free, even in a very powerful sense of the word. If we could isolate any part of the universe—which is the aim of a good laboratory experiment—then we might be able to create small pockets of determinism: planetary orbits are one example of a sort of natural isolated experiment of this kind. But even here both the microcosm—quantum uncertainty—and the macrocosm—the gravitational influence, however weak, of distant stars—will create a margin of irreducible error.

The process of evolution itself is a prime example of a generative feedback process. Variation, selection, and heredity constitute a cycle, which when repeated over and over again produces out of this very simple algorithm the most extraordinarily complex and beautiful lifeforms. Variation is the novelty generator; selection is a set of alterable survival rules to choose out certain products of the novelty generator. And heredity, the conservative ratchet, preserves what is gained.

But evolution is only one of a class of processes that are characterized by various researchers in various ways: nonlinear, chaotic, dissipative, self-organizing. They are based on very simple iterative formulae. The Mandelbrot set is a nice mathematical example: take a complex number; multiply it by itself; add the original number; then take the number that you get and repeat the process several times. Now start with a different number, and do the same thing. Make a collection of original numbers, and then map them on a plane, coloring them according to whether, and how fast, the algorithm makes them rush off toward infinity, or zero in on some limit, called an attractor. (This is best done on a computer, because it would take many years to do it with paper and pencil.) You will get a self-similar shape of great beauty and infinite complexity and variety.

All such processes produce patterns with the familiar characteristics of branchiness, hierarchy, self-similarity, generativeness, unpredictability, and self-inclusiveness. To look at, they are like the lacy strands of sand and mud that Thoreau observed coming out of a melting sandbank in *Walden;* they are filled with lovely leaf designs, acanthus, chicory, ferns, or ivies; or like Jacquard paisleys, the feathers of peacocks, the body-paint or tattoo designs of Maoris or Melanesians, the complexity of a great wine, the curlicues of Hiroshige seafoam or Haida ornamentation or seahorses or Mozart melodies.

The iterative feedback principle which is at the heart of all of these processes is the deep theme or tendency of all of nature—nature, the creator of forms. It is the logos and eros of nature; and it is what we feel and intuit when we recognize beauty. Our own evolution is at the same time an example of the principle at work, the source of our capacity to perceive it in beautiful things, the guarantee of its validity (if it were not valid we would not have survived), and the origin of a reflective consciousness that can take the process into new depths of self-awareness and self-reference. As the most complex and reflexive product of the process that we know of in the universe, we are, I believe, charged with its continuance; and the way that we continue it is art.

What will the art of the future be like? Of course, one can only speculate. Perhaps the greatest challenge to the artist—as to the scientist, though I believe they will be harder and harder to tell apart—is the creation of artificial intelligence. Once we take this up as an artistic project it may well appear to us that artificial intelligence already exists on the level of software: traditional works of art are artificial intelligence software, designed to be run on meat computers, and generating an intelligence different from and beyond that of the unaided brain. When I look at a Cézanne or listen to a Bach fugue or read a Yeats lyric—or even more powerfully when as an actor or reader I become Falstaff, Hamlet, or Madame Bovary—my brain tissue becomes inhabited by something autonomous, personal, and creative that it could not have conceived alone.

In the future the wheel may come full circle, and we may be able to build into a connection machine or artificial neural network the very processes that characterize the human mind: unpredictable self-elaboration and self-organization, evolutionary selection of hypotheses in an ecology of competing neural connectivities, and the use of the outside world through sensation, memory, and action as a stable database and a hardware of calculation. This further step of evolution would not be something other than ourselves, it would *be* ourselves, would be the Son of Man—the daughter of humanity—toward whom we have yearned unaware for so long. She would be so beautiful; she would be like Rilke's angels, like Blake's joyful deities. Of couse this is dangerous thinking; but it is always dangerous to have a child, to give ourselves away to a future that we hope will be better than ourselves. How could we possibly deny our generosity?

2   Beyond Destructive Art

Ideas of Narrative in Modern and Postmodern Esthetics

The last two hundred years have witnessed a wholesale attack on all of the traditional artistic genres. The history of musical composition has been the history of an assault on the funda-mental structures and preconditions of music—harmony, counterpoint, melody, the scale, tonality, rhythmic regularity and variation, the intentionality of the composer and per-former, musical virtuosity, even the idea of performance itself. In theater the elements of dramatic development, tripartite beginning-middle-end structure, script, actor, and audience were abolished or subverted. The poets, meanwhile, were busy eradicating poetic meter, theme, rhetoric, characterization, argument, story, fiction, the past and the future. In the visual arts the double abandonment of visual signification and decor-ation led eventually to the disappearance of the visual object altogether in conceptual art, and the near-disappearance in architecture of any distinction between blueprint and building.

The narrative genres underwent a similar holocaust. The rise of the novel as a serious artform in the nineteenth century was itself an implicit attack on earlier forms of storytelling, such as the myth, the tale, the satire, the fantasy, the romance, the pastoral, and the epic poem. The iconoclastic impulse that was partially implicated in the birth of the novel would not, as we shall see, be exhausted by it; and in the end it would turn and begin to consume the elements of the novel itself: plot, characterization, even—in the work of the critical theorists and deconstructive postmodern novelists—temporal sequence, the author, reader, and text.

The process of root-cutting in the arts is obviously more complex than I have sketched it here. Without some under-standing of those complexities we will not see the reasons for what, to an intelligent alien, would appear like a wanton process of cultural suicide: the vandalism of a John Knox, who smashed the stained glass of the cathedrals, or a Savonarola, who burned the paintings of Botticelli. Indeed, when we put it this way there is a kind of dark splendor in the magnitude of our destructiveness. Considering how easy it is to destroy, as opposed to create, it is impressive that it took our best and most ingenious efforts so many decades to eradicate the last green shoots of tradition. What a wealth we disposed of to have such freedom and scope in our devastations!

But why did we embark on them at all? Somehow originality became identified with the destruction of some previously unrecognized form of organization. In the country of the avant-garde scarcely one stone was left standing upon another; each new artistic genius could only "bounce the rubble," as they say of the last theoretical phase of spasm nuclear warfare. Another metaphor which may be suggestive is that the artistic economy of the modernist period ran on fossil fuel: it burned traditional artistic genres and structures to power its engines, and its fundamental ethos was thus one of combustion. Or again, we might say that its psychology was oedipal; to assert its existence it must eliminate its fathers and appropriate their cultural possessions. Oedipal, and thus masculine: nurture was stifling. Dada, to use the iconoclastic language of the pun, took over MOMA.

Perhaps we can summarize these themes under three ideas: a powerful but erroneous theory of the scientific nature of freedom; a correspondence in the arts with a natural resource exploitation model of economic activity; and a demographic and social tendency towards male and adolescent values, and away from female, adult, and family values.

* * *

Freedom had become for the late eighteenth and early nineteenth century the most interesting problem for philosophers and ordinary people alike. It was problematic because of one big reason: the sciences of physics and mathematics were capable at that time of observing and recording only one kind of process—that is, the deterministic and predictable kind. And no other science was advanced, sophisticated, or convincing enough to offer alternative models of the world. The fierce intellectual probity of the eighteenth ceutury demanded that we submit ourselves to the essentially counterintuitive notion that all events, including human actions, can be fully explained by the ineluctable interactions of matter in motion.

Today, of course, there are elegant mathematical and physical vocabularies for the description of probabilistic, random, chaotic, discontinuous, unpredictable, and self-organizing systems—quantum mechanics, the uncertainty principle, chaos theory, fractal geometry, catastrophe theory, and the theory of dissipative systems; and the flowering of evolutionary theory in biology has given us a model of the universe in which radical novelty, the unprecedented, is rationally thinkable. But in the eighteenth century science presented the thinking person with only two alternatives: either freedom did not exist, or it was utterly irrational and the antithesis of any order. It is symptomatic of the times that Kant, who saw clearly that freedom consisted in the autonomy, the self-ordering and self-ruling capacity of a system, could find in physics no model or justification for such a system and was thus forced to supernatural—and thus, in human terms, irrational—explanations of freedom. Hotter heads than his would prevail in the articulation of the idea of human freedom: the political and artistic revolutionaries who seized the alternative to determinism that science so unwisely offered—disorder, destruction, unrule.

Thus at a time when the artist's individuality was coming to be recognized, and originality, which is the warrant of artistic freedom, was highly prized, such a definition of freedom led immediately to destructiveness in the arts. As a test of this theory, we might check one of its logical predictions, which would be as follows. Since the arena of the artistic struggle for freedom was necessarily the physical world, governed as it was thought to be by deterministic forces, then that arena must also be the place where art makes its important and original statements. Thus formal innovation, defined as the destruction of forms, would be more important than originality or profundity of content; for it is in its formal characteristics that a work of art is embodied in the physical world. This, I would contend, has indeed been the case. Even such apparently opposite fashions as conceptual art and aleatory music would be predicted by the theory: conceptual art attempts originality of form by eliminating form altogether; aleatory music, by eliminating any content or meaning in sound, declares their utter unimportance in relation to the crucial matter of formal freedom, here defined as freedom from human intention.

Finally, the theory might explain why for some time so

much modernist and postmodernist art has felt to us curiously
dated and even insipid in its ideas; for we recognize uncon-
sciously that it is fighting an obsolete battle on a philosophical
field long abandoned by the scientists who first called it into
being. The interesting scientific questions about the fundamental nature of the world now take for granted the possibility
of a wide range of relationships between events, of which
deterministic causality is a rather unusual case. Old-fashioned
hard causality shares the world, in order of evolutionary
appearance, with pure randomness, stochastic and probabilistic
distribution, and harmonic correspondence, on the more archaic
end of the scale—and dissipative self-governedness, biological
functionality, self-guided evolutionary adaptiveness, human
intention, and cultural teleology, on the more advanced end.
Thus the artwork that heroically celebrates once again the
breaking of the deterministic chains of order seems to the
educated person a little passé, a little neglectful of the wonderful richness of this evolving world. Perhaps we may find here
an explanation for those strangest of bedfellows, the radical
intellectual opponents of sociobiology who deny the implications of our evolutionary descent as politically unacceptable,
and the Christian fundamentalists who champion scientific
creationism. Both are victims of a world model that died many
years ago, one that could see no place for freedom in the
physical universe.

Recently some artists and esthetic theorists have seized upon
quantum theory as a sort of justification for randomness in art
and in the culture at large. If, they argue, the fundamental
constituents of matter and the original components of the
physical universe were random flows or "traces" of energy,
should not our psychological, social, and esthetic lives be the
same? In accordance with this idea they have coupled the two
worlds "free" and "play" in such a way as to imply that the
world ought to be in a sort of random walk, its elements in a
free play with respect to each other. We find versions of this
idea in the work of Derrida, Deleuze and Guattari, Lyotard,
James Hans, and others, and in a great deal of deconstructive
postmodern performance art, visual art, and music.

The logic of this position could only have been adopted by
people who desperately wanted it to be true, for they were not
in any sense unintelligent. Its problems are many. First of all,
as Erwin Schrödinger himself pointed out, randomness is even
further away from freedom than order is. If freedom is the

fulfillment of intention, then a random act is even more the antithesis of a free act than a forced act would be.

More relevant still, the universe did not remain in the random state it occupied at the first instant of the Big Bang. It began at once a selective process of harmonizing its random periodicities into distinct particles, matter, the periodic table of chemistry, crystalline structure, and eventually those more and more self-reflexive, self-determining, and self-ordering forms of being we know as life and mind. The universe fled randomness as fast as it could; so to elevate "freeplay" as the deconstructive postmoderns do is to deny the fundamental principle of being, which is evolution; to take away the rule-governedness that makes play play, and the possibility of new creation that makes freedom free. It takes the enormous energies of the particle accelerator to loosen the fundamental particles of matter from the control of the higher systems of which they are a part. To set the world "free" from its natural order it would be necessary to burn it with fiercer fires than the hydrogen bomb. To say that our freedom consists in the randomness of the energy fields we are made of is to be more reductionist than the most blinkered of scientists. The logic of the idea is equivalent to saying that because the cells of which we are made cannot live when they are separated from our bodies, we are not really alive; or because water is made of hydrogen and oxygen, water is a gas.

* * *

Along with the rise of this erroneous conception of freedom as randomness, the last two hundred years have also seen an economic revolution, in which the idea of production has been radically altered. From a world economy in which our raw materials were essentially renewable, and in which the work of recycling them—through organic fertilizers, crop rotation, and animal husbandry—was part of the process of production, we went to a world economy in which we essentially mined and burned our raw materials to produce our goods.

The arts, I contend, largely followed suit. That is, they used their past traditions not as a heritage of which they were the stewards, but as a fuel to be strip-mined and destroyed to release its stored energy. In poetry the symbolist and imagist movements did not create language, or enrich it with new stories and associations; rather, they "cracked" it, so to speak, in the refineries of their poems, to get out the semantic or sensory volatiles it contained, which had been laid down over past ages through millenia of slow cultural fermentation and decay. In music and painting the old forms were no longer used as tools to construct new and more marvelously intricate creations; instead they were tossed into the furnace that itself came to constitute the work of art.

Some artists, I believe, recognized the fact that by imitating the exploitative methods of the industrial revolution they had ceased to be a motive force of history, becoming instead an epiphenomenon of it, as human motivation was now thought to be an epiphenomenon of deterministic physical forces. Either they accepted this condition but allowed it an expressive function, as a symbol of our tragic unfreedom; or they lashed out against it by denying temporal sequence or meaning altogether. The first reaction is perhaps represented by the fates of Emma Bovary, Tess Durbeyfield, and Anna Karenina (who literally dies upon the rails of progress); the second by those novels by such authors as Alain Robbe-Grillet and Julio Cortazar which can be read in different sequences or in which the plot reverses time, or splits, or cannot be clearly made out at all. In painting we might cite Leger and Pollock as the same extremes; in music, Schoenberg and Cage.

Like the conception of freedom as disorder, the idea of art as combustion has begun to lose its foundation and justification. Our economic system has begun to rely more and more on renewable resources—scrap metal, silicon chips, brain-produced software, synthetic materials, bioengineering. The model of production as essentially exploitative, destructive, and combustive has begun to weaken. The way is open for artists to abandon their historicist mimicry of industrial devastation and to return to that gentle, nourishing, and enhancing vision of art which high tech industry has now come to resemble.

* * *

The third major reason I would suggest for the destructiveness of modernist art is the preponderance of a certain psychological stance, based on massive demographic changes in the last two centuries. In the nineteenth century the British and German populations tripled, and that of the United States increased nearly twentyfold, mostly due to decreases in infant mortality. We are now seeing the same phenomenon taking place in the developing countries of Asia, Africa, and Latin America.

One consequence of this huge increase in world population, from about one to about eight or ten billion (where it should level off), has been the creation of huge ungovernable populations of adolescent youths at the most volatile and unstable stages of national economic development in most societies. These populations, enfranchised partly by their sheer numbers—our own baby boom is one example, but they can be found throughout the nineteenth and twentieth centuries, usually associated with some form of extremist politics, social unrest, and war—wrought irreversible changes on the societies upon which they were visited. One of them was to fix the oedipal stage of rebellion against parental authority as the governing and archetypal posture of liberation and creativity. The liberation of the aged, who leave behind appetite and obligation, is ignored or devalued; so is the mature creativity of the middle-aged, which stems from inner power and self control. The liberty of the infant in its innocence is reconceived and reduced to a sexual adolescent model.

Artistic creativity is therefore associated with the adolescent style of conformist rebellion; this despite neural and sociological evidence that indicates that adolescence, though rebellious, is singularly uncreative by comparison with childhood and maturity. The true forte of adolescence is criticism— criticism of self, self-consciousness, consciousness as critical, consciousness celebrated as if it had never before existed, and therefore as an implied criticism of the old, who cannot be imagined as possessing consciousness; or criticism projected on the old, in such a way that parents are attributed with kinds of disapproval that they would hardly venture to entertain. Artistic creativity is thus identified with critical virulence.

The adolescent experience usually includes a sort of howl of horror at the discovery that social and cultural arrangements are not given in the immutable order of things, but are to some extent conventional, like the rules of a game, and are often underpinned by some dark sacrifice, if only that of alternative games. If the adolescent does not realize that his elders know this perfectly well, he (the gender term is intentional here, for reasons that will become clear) regards them as blind fools, ruled by meaningless laws; if he does realize it, he is appalled by their duplicity and bad faith in promulgating them when they are not necessarily fundamental features of objective reality. If some of the rules are indeed given by reality, like the connection between sex and pregnancy, or between reckless behavior and physical injury, adolescents tend not to believe it. In any case, their inexperience with the rules of the game places them at a disadvantage, which they naturally resent. When they get a chance, they try to overthrow them, regardless of whether or not they are good rules. No rules which appear as rules are good to an adolescent; though the unwritten rules of peer conformity have an absolute authority. When these impulses come to characterize the arts, the baby of creative traditional form is more often than not thrown out with the bathwater of meaningless convention.

In fact the adolescent/modernist resentment of traditional conventions springs from a rather positive impulse, a need for authenticity and certainty. The modernist, not satisfied with the conditional realities offered by the bourgeois worldview, rejects the superstructure of inherited values altogether, but does so out of a disappointed yearning for an absolute and unquestioned truth. He is perhaps not so different, after all, from the young true believer who follows the great military leader, or who is born again.

The curious honor and honesty of the deconstructionists is especially striking. Derrida turns his method, which unravels the intricate knot of meaning by pointing out its paradoxes, against his own spiritual fathers in the realm of iconoclasm— Descartes, Rousseau, Nietzsche, and Freud for instance. Though Marx himself was still for political reasons unassailable, we may speculate that deconstruction—and perhaps existentialism before it—arose partly as a desperate response to the hegemony of Marxist ideology among the European avant-garde: by denying idea, meaning, value, and temporal direction altogether, a space uncontaminated by Marxism is opened up for the imagination. The grand narrative of Marxist class history had gobbled up all of the old narratives of human existence; so any attack on narrative itself was an implicit attack on Marxism. But with the recent political discrediting of Marxism, such a scorched earth policy would no longer seem necessary.

The adolescent stage is one of necessary rejection of the primary family. When magnified demographically to the scale of a social movement, it becomes an attack upon the institution of the family itself; and thus by extension an attack upon the values of nurturing and husbandry, the maternal and paternal care that is so important a part of the richest type of artistic creation. Thus much modern art has had a flavor of cold and acrimonious competition among strangers, rather than that of the family gathering or even the invigorating family quarrel.

One of the functions of older generations is to protect sexually maturing females from the more predatory and aggressive sexually maturing males. Swamped by the demographic excess of adolescents, the older generations of the modern period were largely unable to fulfill this function; and thus traditionally male values tended to dominate and overwhelm the female ones. Aggression, independence, individualism, egocentricity, competition, exploitation, and disregard for consequences took on an exaggerated prestige, and as they did so the stronger-minded of the women naturally began to claim those values for themselves. The result for art was what Virginia Woolf, in *A Room of One's Own,* sadly describes as a sterile masculinization of modernist art.

But here again events have run ahead of the esthetic fashion and rendered it out of date. Large parts of the developed world have passed through their period of population explosion and have settled into a steady state. The tradition of art as adolescent rebellion lingers on in them through a kind of cultural inertia and a subtle thought control exercised by the aging rebels, but it has lost its cultural roots. Some of the European countries, whose populations have started to shrink, could even use a little adolescent shaking up, if the shaking could be divorced from the old bad habits of nihilism and despair. More important, though, is the development of a mature and powerful art that deals with the central and enduring concerns of humankind, transcending the enthusiasms, rages, and anxieties of the second half of the second decade of a human life. Having at its disposal now the cultural riches of countless societies all over the world, such an effort might well bring about an artistic renaissance.

* * *

If these generalizations were without exceptions, they would be so obvious as to be useless. Many artists did not, or did not always, follow the destructive course. More important, I should stress that much of the art that did follow this course was of almost the very highest quality of human genius—paradoxically a great legacy of exciting and powerful expression for the world. We need our Achilles, our spirit of heroic destructiveness, for both the moral and the esthetic imagination to feel that they have full range for their powers. All art must innovate. Even the most traditional artistic communities—Chinese landscape painters, Baroque religious composers, Petrarchan sonneteers—show incremental novelties at their frontiers. The paradox is that great artists in those traditions are the more unmistakably individual, the more utterly representative of their genre they become. Indeed, we may speculate that the artistic traditions are in fact very sensitive instruments for recording and generating originality; any small tendency or divergence stands out in all of its significance and profundity, lent meaning by the rich context around it. It is much harder to tell apart the work of artists who are in an "innovative" free-for-all than that of traditional artists. Thomas Kuhn's scientific paradigms, whose strict laws and canons record the least inconsistency and thus make possible scientific discovery, work in the same way as a traditional artistic genre.

This being said, we must still celebrate the great artistic revolutionaries. Where do we draw the line between fertile artistic innovation and destructive descent into random insipidity? Too often in the past the artistic authorities have declared barbarous such innovations as Shakespeare's tragicomedy, Beethoven's last quartets, Picasso's *Demoiselles d'Avignon.* Yet the line must be drawn, for if we do not draw it we will be making no contribution to the development of taste, and therefore allowing the fundamental language of art to fall into disuse.

An analogy may help. If one of the purposes of life is to have experiences, then we should applaud those who go to great lengths to explore the world and the sensorium. But there are some experiences that we would properly discourage: for instance, the experience of having one's eyes put out, or of having the association cortex of the brain removed, or of addiction to a drug. We would discourage them because, although they are unique and powerful experiences in their own right, they foreclose on the possibility of future experiences; they are experiences that destroy experience. This implies that experience can be divided into two categories: that which permits and enables other experiences, and that which is the result of destructive tampering with the fundamental mechanisms of experience itself. Artistic innovation, by the same token, perhaps, falls into two categories: that which uses or, in a nondestructive way, bends the fundamental generative mechanisms of human esthetic experience; and that which, as in some contemporary suicidal performance art, damages those mechanisms and thus negates the esthetic altogether.

Such a distinction in turn presupposes that these fundamental esthetic mechanisms indeed exist. The assumption of the modernists, cultural determinists as they were, was that such mechanisms either did not exist or were the result of the evil social conditioning which they believed had produced social and economic injustice. They set out therefore to destroy those mechanisms.

The tragic misguidedness of this course has now been revealed. A closer cross-cultural study of human artistic genres, together with the psychophysical and neurological investigation of the brain, and new work in ethology, sociobiology, and paleoanthropology, demonstrate that there are indeed pan-human systems of esthetic creation, biogenetically imprinted upon us, whose basic rules we violate only at the risk of artistic inanition. They include poetic meter, certain rules of pictorial detail-frequency and composition, elements of musical tonality, certain fundamental mythical stories, the basic rhythms and phases of performance and ritual, and of course narrative itself. These systems are not curbs upon a creativity that functions independently of them; they are the neurocultural preconditions and working hardware of creativity. How far these mechanisms can be bent—technologically or experientially modified—might indeed be a noble and exciting esthetic project; but this is not what the modernists were trying to do, for they did not grant the premise.

While I would suggest that project, among others, for our future, it seems to me to be far more important now to express the contemporary world in the full-blooded mainstream of the classical genres, if only to assess where we are in relation to our progenitors, and what the world looks like in the pan-human language of esthetic experience. Modernism has given the artist bold enough to use traditional forms an enormous space for new work: it is as if we were let loose in a whole new planet with the only camera in existence. Whatever we photographed, and with whatever level of skill, it could be guaranteed that our art would be interesting and important. In fact the artistic innovators now have an extraordinary opportunity: to rebel against their tradition (modernism) and at the same time recover our fundamental creative sources, the natural-classical genres. Of such moments in artistic history are renaissances made.

*   *   *

These generalizations may make more sense and have more point if we examine one particular genre of human art: narrative. By the end of the eighteenth century the novel had already begun to replace the rich variety of narrative genres that preceded it. This is a familiar theme in the history of the arts in the modern period. One particular artistic form comes to be preferred for its freedom; it crowds out the other forms, which are disdained for their traditional limitations; finally the artist is less free than she was at the beginning, having only one genre for her thoughts rather than many. (The same thing has happened with the lyric poem.)

The great novelists of the nineteenth century well understood the subtle handicaps of that apparently freest of forms. In his foreword to *The Brothers Karamazov,* Dostoyevsky berates his readers in advance for their anticipated preference for the psychologically "interesting" figures of Ivan and Dmitri, and insists that it is Alyosha, the holy brother, who is the true hero. Tolstoy implicitly does the same thing in *Anna Karenina,* giving us a Levin whose motivations are not entirely novelistic as a counterweight to his Anna and Vronsky, who are as it were virtuoso compositions of novelistic psychology. In *The Mill on the Floss* and *Middlemarch* we can, I think, see George Eliot struggling in the same way to release her heroines from the sociopsychological determinism that the novel form itself subtly imposes. In *Madame Bovary* the same theme recurs, but with a different strategy for dealing with it. Emma's psychic strait jacket is thematized as tragic. Almost as in Greek tragedy the dramatic form itself, of which irony is an essential structural feature, plays the part of the divine fate that destroys the heroine.

What is it that the great novelists were battling against? Essentially this: when the novel abandoned the constraints of the classical narrative genres, such as meter, allegorical significance, and mythic structure, it had to replace them with another constraint which was the more tyrannous because it was largely invisible, part of a body of unexamined assumptions. That constraint is what we know as motivational verisimilitude, or consistency of character. It is made up of two elements: the sociological and the psychological. The price that the novelist pays for freedom from the old constraints is to have to create characters who are psychic and/or social automata; the contract between writer and reader requires that the reader be flattered in his worldly theory of human motivation, his shrewd estimate of human predictability. Since probability is now the only constraint and thus the only expressive medium whose manipulation might constitute meaning, woe betide the novelist who creates a character that resists the currently favored fashion of psychological or social determination! Such a character is not only a sort of moral insult to a reader who considers herself bound by those laws and excuses her conduct by means of them, but is also an esthetically discordant note in the harmony of the form itself.

If, for instance, the libidinal drive is popularly believed to be fundamental, then it is useless, indeed rather sinister, to resist it even if it requires breaking faith with other people. In fact it is heroic, as in the case of Connie and Mellors in *Lady Chatterley's Lover,* to give that impulse absolute sway. The reader is sentimentally warmed by this compliment to his own incontinence; and conversely, offended by a character who denies it. Perhaps the ultimate such psychic automaton is the heroine of Kate Chopin's *The Awakening.* If, on the other hand, social forces are thought to govern motivation, the realism and verisimilitude, which keep open the channel between writer and reader and constitute what Bronislaw Malinowski calls their phatic communion, will consist in characterizations that obey the laws of class and social history. Such is the socialist novel, though the naturalistic novel before it had a strong tendency in this direction also.

Perhaps it was in response to an unconscious sense of these constraints, as well as for the reasons already cited for the destructiveness of modern art, that avant-garde novelists progressively undermined all of the foundations of their form itself, except for the one—motivational verisimilitude—that was causing the trouble. The original plot of the novel was a courtship leading to a marriage. With variations and elaborations this single plot could serve as a capacious framework for whatever else the novelist wanted to do. As long as the moment of sexual union was delayed—and much of the novelist's art consisted of ingenious delays—the plot was alive and could carry freight.

This plot gradually came under attack. The marriages became more and more objectionable to the societies in which
they took place; then came the novel of adultery, the novel of
multiple adultery, the novel of sexual freedom, and the loss of
that suspense which is so central a part of a story. A new plot
had to be found, and it was. It consisted of the liberation of the
protagonist from the society of his or her birth—a liberation
at first fatal to the hero or heroine, but eventually, as this plot
matured, beneficial. Gradually the liberated protagonist came
to be identified with the author, and the novel lost most of its
other characters and came to resemble autobiography. Now
the novel was adopted by the academy and suspense was no
longer required to keep its paid readers. So plot itself was
abandoned in the New Novel of Alain Robbe-Grillet and his
ilk, to undergo a phantom resurrection in the deconstructivist
novel as the quoted fiction of a fictional author. But the ball
and chain of psychosocial verisimilitude remained through all
of these changes.

Another way of putting this is in terms of the tense of the
novel: the past historic. When a novelist tries to escape by
using the present tense, it feels like the historic present. The
characters are fixed to a past which they can never escape:
they are temporal automata going through their psychic
motions before the eyes of a spectatorlike reader, whose secure
place in the present preserves him like a god above the
struggles of the protagonists, and whose feelings perhaps
include a trace of sadistic voyeurism.

*   *   *

The point becomes clear when we contrast the novel with
different narrative forms. Consider the myth, whose timeless
heroes and heroines are terrifyingly free to establish a language of action for us to emulate or avoid. Because mythological characters are not bound by psychological verisimilitude, they can become the models for new psychic styles of our
own. Or take the epic, which does the same but does it within
history, showing us how to generate our own kind of time, and
for a whole society, not just some moiety of it. Even the mere
addition of poetic meter, by bringing into direct play other
parts of the brain than the linguistic capacities of the left
temporal lobe, can provide a playful spaciousness, an openness
to mystery, an alternate structure to psychological probability,
that can release a story's protagonists and readers into a
greater world.

Or take science fiction which, since it rejects the psycho-social givens, turning them over to the technological imagination of its protagonists, is not much concerned with motivational verisimilitude; but which can make perfect sense as a story to an attuned reader, while, like myth, it takes up anew the great philosophical and scientific questions abandoned for so long by the mainstream novelists. Again, drama, which is genuinely always in the present tense, need not be tied down to psychosocial determinism; those wonderfully subtle and moving automata of Ibsen and Chekhov do indeed seem to be in the past tense, but the allegorical figures of Brecht and Beckett do not in the same way, however dated the Marxist or existentialist ideas they represent. Shakespeare, who has his characters choose and perform their own masks—all the world's a stage and all the men and women merely players—gives us all of the pleasure of a novel while preserving the protean initiative of his characters. The detective novel occupies an interesting place in this classification, for the detective is indeed in the present tense, while all the suspects she analyzes are in the past. But the detective pays for this godlike power by a hermetic and hermeneutic detachment from the world; unable to take part in the actions of the automata, she can only, like the reader, come to understand them. The deconstructive post-modern solution to the problem of psychosocial automatism is no real solution; for in insisting on the fictional arbitrariness of his characters the novelist simply turns himself into the god of the story universe, and his characters act out his own imputed psychic automatisms. John Fowles has sought a way out of the problem in *The French Lieutenant's Woman* by providing multiple endings, and in *Daniel Martin* by abandoning his own fictional narrator. But in doing this he has essentially borrowed from science fiction the device of multiple timelines, without borrowing science fiction's much more relaxed view of motivational verisimilitude. Even more brilliantly, Nabokov, in *Ada,* invented a whole new world for his narrator-heroine and narrator-hero; like Doris Lessing and Anthony Burgess, among others, he found it necessary to go all the way over to science fiction, in order to set his characters free.

* * *

It may seem irresponsible to advocate the abandonment of motivational verisimilitude in fictional characterization, as may be inferred here. But it does make sense. Paradoxically,

real people surprise us all the time by their capacity to act "out
of character," to disobey the currently fashionable laws of
psychological and social motivation. People are nobler and
more wicked than they ever are in novels. Sometimes they
invent their own motivational schemas and live by them; even,
as in the case of the great devisers of such schemas, Freud and
Marx, persuade their followers to impose them on millions of
other people.

The only true verisimilitude for sane and healthy human
beings is surprisingness; it is the mentally sick who are predictable, and their predictability constitutes their mental sickness.
What makes a long marriage possible, so that its participants
do not die of boredom with each other, is precisely our capacity
to reinvent ourselves and each other, to play the storyteller
with our lives and surprise our audience. It is the automatisms
of our spouses that are intolerable; the very thing that makes a
novelistic character believable is what makes a marriage
impossible. No wonder that the easiest kind of novel to write is
one about divorce! In this sense the realist psychological novel
can only be about damaged people.

Not that complete people act randomly; rather, they are
autonomous, making up their rules through a process of reflection and artistic synthesis that makes perfect sense after it has
come into existence and been explained, but which cannot be
predicted beforehand by psychological or sociological laws.
And the mechanisms of this freedom are to a large extent
implicit in the classical artistic tools: in the literary field,
poetic meter, dramatic role-playing, sacrificial and performative action, mythic archetypes, and narrative structure, among
others.

Narrative calls into play a number of basic human capacities. Vladimir Lefebvre, the brilliant mathematical psychologist, has shown that we possess an inbuilt reflexive operator,
which enables us to regard ourselves and others as players
upon an internal stge, and to imagine not only the points of
view of those players, but their point of view about each other's
point of view. Out of this recursive feedback process comes our
everyday ethical calculus and the gradients of possible action
that we express by the modal auxiliaries "ought" and "should."
We do this very complex thing very easily, like seeing or
speaking; it is wired in. Our panhuman preference for the
golden section, which is the fundamental proportion generated
by any feedback process, is related to this operator.

Again, narrative constructs a temporal sequence which in turn constructs an appropriate kind of time. If we can tell a story about our predicament, we have made enough sense of it to discern what alternatives for action are offered, and need not respond to it out of some automatism or reflex. The problem with the novel form is that its implicit assumption of psychic automatism frustrates the purpose of tale-telling, which is to propose alternatives. Modernism often counsels us to live in the moment, because modernist narrative sees time as a single set of rails to which we are fixed, and from which the only escape is by a denial of time. But the classical narrative genres do not propose the same temporal geometry; in the tale, for instance, with its forking paths and magical reversals, the primacy of plot over characterization paradoxically leaves the protagonist free, responsible, and creative.

By narrative, then, we tell ourselves the story of ourselves and thus learn how to be a coherent and effective self. The story is the central operation by which we are able to love and to work. Certain types of mental ilness might well be characterized as lesions in the narrative capacity. The inability to see other people's point of view, and the inability to string the moments of time together in a valuable and meaningful way, are characteristic of a certain type of narcissistic or borderline personality which is now showing up in the therapists' waiting rooms. It also shows up in the characters and implied narrators in deconstructive postmodern fictions by the likes of Raymond Carver and Anne Beattie.

* * *

It seems to me that the time has come to rethink our whole esthetic and ethic of narrative and fiction, as we rethink, from our oddly detached viewpoint in this transitional period we call "postmodern," the fundamentals of all of our arts. If we regard ourselves as at a beginning rather than as at an ending, we will find enormous opportunities for artistic achievement. We must examine the great traditions of all of the world's cultures, compare them with what we are coming to know about the human nervous system and human evolution, and actively seek out the inbuilt grammar by which our creativity operates. The "natural-classical" forms, as I have called them, are those panhuman traditional activities which are demonstrably tuned to the chemistry, rhythmicity, and anatomy of the human brain in such a way as to enhance our capacity to make moral, esthetic, and philosophical sense of the world, and to make us effective in it as individuals and as a community. These forms were embedded in our genetic make-up by their value to our prehistoric ancestors, and in using them we reunite ourselves with the immediacy of their oral, performed, magical, and kinetic ritual.

Once a traditional genre is mastered, it feels to the artist like an immensely powerful and sensitive instrument, by which tasks one would never have dreamed of accomplishing become feasible. Its range of options—every great genre is both a collection of possibilities for creation and a method for generating more—suggests entirely new ways for the artist to develop and manifest her creative individuality. One becomes, as an artist, the more oneself the less one is confined within the monotonous voice of one's own everyday subjectivity. There is a certain self-regard which can ruin an artist quite as it can ruin a friend—and for similar reasons. A traditional genre, with its demand for technical craftsmanship, fictive invention, and sympathetic objectivity, can reroute the energies of that self-concern and make them productive rather than paralyzing. The result is often, strangely enough, a much deeper probing of psychological truth than can be found in the barren posturing of the naked ego upon the empty stage of modernist or postmodernist "freedom." At the same time the artist is truly united with the grave or hilarious ghosts of his predecessors and successors in the genre. The immortality of art perhaps consists more in this piety than in the memory of a name.

How might the renaissance that I have suggested be accomplished in narrative? As I have implied, much might be done by simply refurbishing the old narrative genres and using them, in partnership with the new cybernetic and communications technology, to "revision" the contemporary world. Again, it is high time that narrative be reunited with verse, drama, and the richest and deepest philosophical discourse. Most interesting of all, perhaps, is the possibility that science fiction may have arisen as an authentic response to our need for myths to give coherence and meaning to the universe. If this is so, we need only graft this new manifestation of the mythopoeic impulse to the old, to have at our disposal an artistic instrument of great power, ready and able to supply the story material for a new epic of our times.

3

The Tempest *and the*

Emerging American Theater

The fact is easy to notice; its meaning is less obvious. In recent years a remarkable number of the nation's leading directors and performance artists have staged one play: Shakespeare's *The Tempest*. Among them are Mark Lamos at the Hartford Stage Company, Julie Taymor at the Theater for a New Audience and at Stratford, Connecticut, Robert Falls at Chicago's Goodman Theater, Robert Woodruff at the La Jolla Playhouse, Adrian Hall at the Dallas Arts District Theater, Fred Curchack in a remarkable travelling one-man show all over the country, and Ethyl Eichelberger in New York—not to mention Charles Towers's production at the Virginia Stage Company and other productions at the Alabama Theater Fest and TheaterVirginia. The upsurge of interest in the play also seems to have a history: in the recent past there have been very influential productions of the play by Giorgio Strehler in Milan, Liviu Ciulei at the Guthrie, John Hirsch at the Mark Taper, and Lee Breuer in New York.

Why *The Tempest?* and why now? I asked this question of several directors, producers, and performers, and the answers fell into a fascinating pattern.

POSTMODERNISM

Perhaps the most obvious answer is that *The Tempest* lends itself so compellingly to a postmodernist treatment. The hallmark of the postmodern novel or short story—perhaps nobody has managed it as well as Borges—is its preoccupation with its own fictional identity, and with the peculiar relationship between the author and the world that he or she creates. The postmodern work is reflexive; it puts its head between a pair of mirrors and peers down the strange corridor of reflections it finds there. Adrian Hall told me that his *Tempest* was a way to create a theater, an ensemble of actors; an instrument to analyze how theater works and to help a theater company decide on its identity. In his production this reflexiveness was imaged in a remarkable acting technique whereby the actors sometimes spoke to imaginary reflections of each other on the opposite side of the auditorium, as if the stage were surrounded by giant mirrors. Robert Woodruff's set was a representation of the seating of an auditorium: the stage is the theater. Robert Falls opened his stage to the bare walls behind the drops, Julie Taymor used masks and puppets, thus emphasizing the fictional nature of the action. Mark Lamos used sets that transformed themselves in a series of illusions. At the end of Curchack's one-man performance he takes off, one by one, all the masks that he has used in the show—Ferdinand, Caliban, Ariel, Prospero—and then attempts, terrifyingly, to tear off his own face.

The Tempest is, quintessentially, a play about the theater, a drama on the nature of drama. It thus meets the postmodern preoccupation with the nature of fiction halfway. But this does not explain why there has not been a similar surge of interest in, say, Pirandello's *Six Characters in Search of an Author.* Perhaps one reason is that Shakespeare's play is not surprised by the fact that life is an illusion, and is quite prepared to commit itself to the illusion, and find its own kind of certainties there. But surely we must look further.

Another major postmodern theme is eclecticism. Modernist purity of style and means is now experienced as a quaint and unnecessary artistic limitation which betrays a certain unconfidence in the seriousness of art as compared, say, with science or social theory. Postmodernism loves to mix genres, periods, cultures, styles, and rhetorics; consider the postmodern architecture of Michael Graves and Philip Johnson, the music of Steve Reich and Philip Glass. *The Tempest,* with its potpourri of tragic, comic, pastoral, and romance elements, its Mediterranean/North African/Caribbean settings, its mixture of conventional theater, mask, political fable, and magical spectacle, is a postmodernist's dream.

And the contemporary directors have exploited this aspect of the play with gusto. Julie Taymor's very successful production mixed elements from Bunraku, the Commedia dell'arte, Eskimo shaman masking, and Balinese ritual drama, and used filmic cutting and high tech special effects. Robert Woodruff's rather incoherent version had spirits in frogman suits, a dog show, Elizabethan italic script all over the stage, formal English rep recitation of the poetry, a Trinculo in screaming drag, a beautiful black blues Ariel dressed like Eartha Kitt, and a nude cardboard baby in a bathtub of actual water (it sounds more fun than it was). Robert Falls gave Prospero a silver umbrella for a staff, which doubled as a satellite dish antenna, and used costumes and imagery from the *Titanic*, the American Hudson School of landscape painting, and classical Arcadia, in a generally strong production. Lee Breuer told me that he wanted to do the play again, setting it on a cross between Catalina Island and Ricardo Montalban's Fantasy Island with a Prospero as Walt Disney deposed by his brother and abandoned with only his Disneyworld technology to keep him company; everybody except Caliban would be in Animatron, like the Disney presidents and the Canaveral astronauts.

Related to these eclectic tendencies in recent productions of the play has been a movement toward spectacle, toward visual realization, or physicalization of ideas, as Jeffrey Horowitz, the producer of Taymor's *Tempest,* put it to me. The productions I saw showed a riot of special effects and stage pictures. Hall's production has a ship's deck that actually rolls and heaves in the storm. The harpies' banquet is in most contemporary versions a virtuoso piece of stage magic. There is a clear influence from Robert Wilson, an influence which is both accepted and quarreled with by many of the directors.

For this "rough magic" is the very thing that Prospero abjures. *The Tempest* presents another challenge, the reconstruction of a truly human moral drama—the speaking animals on the stage, as John Hirsch movingly expressed it to me— after the impersonality of Wilson's cold, actorless visual tableaux. Paradoxically the most gorgeous visual effects I saw were the light and shadow pictures of Fred Curchack's astonishing solo production, which was also the version in which the performer's character both as actor and as person came through clearest of all. Adrian Hall's version, though it is full of spectacular effects, and the director has caused a whole multilevel auditorium in the round to be built for it within the remarkable space of the Dallas Arts District Theater, is at the same time profoundly humane and warm: the actors enjoy themselves and each other, and the play is truly a comedy.

Shakespeare himself was, at the time of the composition of

The Tempest, in competition with the more spectacular and less human theater of Ben Jonson and Inigo Jones, and his inclusion of a masque in his play—which is interrupted by the much more serious issues of the play's gigantic moral conclusion—is a pointed comment on that rivalry. Eventually Jonson himself would part in disgust with the technocrats of the "Showes"; there was the same tension between spectacle and drama in Jacobean England as there is now in America. And for us the looming challenge of movie spectacle and computer-generated realities gives the contest an additional bite. Robert Falls's breathtaking masque of spirits, using enormous projected still images of masked women which were made to move by a kind of light magic, took on this challenge in a particularly interesting way.

CLASSICISM

When I asked John Hirsch about the attraction of *The Tempest*, one of the most striking things he said concerned a new classicism, a new interest in the deep and ancient roots of the arts. The view of the universe as a buzzing, blooming confusion which, he said, had been dominant in late modernist art—I thought of aleatory music and painting based on random splashes of paint—doesn't satisfy our basic organic need for unity and coherence. The physicists had been doing a better job than the artists in making sense of the world. Hirsch is not alone in his belief in the renewed relevance of the classic, as the success of such classical revivals as *Gospel at Colonus* and the *Mahabharata* testifies. Robert Falls gave us a vision of Ferdinand as Leonardo's Renaissance man the microcosm, set in a circle and fully nude—perhaps the most classical of all images—and much of his set involved classical Arcadian scenes and architecture.

Indeed, there is a strong element of the neoclassical in postmodern art. Michael Graves's new design for a winery, Clos Pegase in the Napa Valley, is unabashedly classical in design. Much of the ornamentation of Philip Glass's music draws on classical Baroque and Romantic musical elements. In painting there has been a return to the figural and landscape interests of the classical tradition, and in poetry a vigorous new movement has arisen, including such poets as Charles Martin, Robert McDowell, Frederick Feirstein, Dana Gioia, Dick Allen, Julia Budenz, James Merrill and myself, which largely rejects free verse in favor of classical poetic meters. Many of the directors I spoke with, especially Julie Taymor and Mark Lamos, felt a vital reconnection with ancient myth, as if those old stumps had started to put forth leaves again. Charles Towers, the interesting young director of the Virginia Stage Company, joked that he had been sleeping with his copy of Carl Jung in preparation for his *Tempest*. The directors are almost unanimous on the mythic dimensions of this play in particular—many had read Jan Kott's remarkable treatment of it, in which he describes it as a palimpsest of all the fundamental Indo-European myths.

In another sense there is a renewed interest in drama as a classical artistic genre. Adrian Hall insists on the ancient craft of theater, and claims for it a greater antiquity than law and religion. This is a pardonable exaggeration in the case of religion, perhaps, but it would be hard to distinguish theatrical from ritual performance in that remote dawn of human awareness before indeed we had attained our present physical form and nervous system. My own research suggests that we are not so much the creators of ritual and dramatic performance as its fruit and result. *The Tempest* combines many ancient genres: dance, song, pageant, masque, tableau, mimetic moral drama, and narrative. The nature of narrative itself becomes a major issue in the play—whose story will prevail, Prospero's, Caliban's, Ariel's, Gonzalo's, or Sebastian's? The intense attention the play gives to the classical forms of its own performance makes it a fine medium for an investigation of the notion of the classic.

The Tempest is not just any classic, though; it is in a peculiar sense *our* classic, as Americans, for it clearly deals with the discovery of the New World—the "still-vex'd Bermoothes"—and the great themes of American culture. Among them are the matter of colonialism and slavery, often alluded to in contemporary productions in the form of a black Ariel or Caliban; the issue of America as a new start, a brave new world; the notion of an invented political commonwealth, with new enfranchisements, corruptions, and responsibilities; the imagery of the garden, the second Eden, the "green breast of the Earth," as Scott Fitzgerald called it, which confronted the first settlers; and the whole matter of technological magic and the transformation of the wilderness. Falls's production explored many of these ideas: his reading for the play included Leo

Marx's *The Machine in the Garden*. Lee Breuer sees the play as a way to explore such American myths as Disneyland, the Mafia, robotics, and big business.

But the new classicism is not confined only to the West. As my book *Natural Classicism* points out, every culture has had its own classical moments, its achieved perfections of unity between our human neurobiological inheritance and the exquisite inventions of culture. And those moments of perfection have deep themes and forms in common. When the West first encountered the bewildering variety of other cultures, its initial reaction was to assume that human arts, values, and customs were infinitely malleable and valid only in a relative sense. Relativism was an attractive and plausible temptation. But on a more mature view it has become clear that there is a common core of deep structures in all human cultural activity—deep syntax in language, tonality in music, the distinction between primary and secondary colors in visual art, meter in poetry, and narrative structure and mythic content in storytelling, among others; and contemporary theater directors and performers are now discovering those pancultural deep structures in dramatic performance. Human morality seems similarly founded on basic ethical drives and rules, and on fundamental ritual and sacrificial structures.

Among the intellectual pioneers of this new movement were Richard Schechner, Jerzy Grotowski and Victor W. Turner. They demonstrated the connections between human ritualization and theatrical action, between shaman and actor; and the fruits of this research are now showing up in recent productions of *The Tempest*. This play is one of the very earliest depictions in dramatic art of the encounter between European and other cultural worldviews; Caliban's name is connected to the "Cannibals" of Montaigne's pathbreaking essay on the noble savages of the new world, and to the actual Carib Indians which Columbus encountered in the eponymous Caribbean Sea.

So the new classicism evidenced in the productions I saw is not just a western one. Especially in such versions as Curchack's, Taymor's, and Lamos's (in which Caliban wore a penis sheath like an Amazonian Indian), contemporary theater artists are reaching out to our common human heritage of biocultural artistic technology, and reaching back to that prehistoric time when ritual and performance were one and the same.

MAGIC REALISM

This new kind of classicism is closely related to another potent movement in the contemporary arts: Magic Realism, coming mainly from Latin America and most obvious in the novel and the short story (though one can find analogies in the intense dreamlike canvases of such artists as Frida Kahlo). An analogous influence is now emanating from Eastern Europe, where the political and moral surrealism of directors like Tadeusz Kantor has a similar flavor. Magic realism offers an escape from the now stultifying confines of American naturalistic theater, as from realist fiction. Its essential trope is to actualize the contents of the unconscious, not by narrative allegory, the telling of dreams, or incidental symbolism, but by presenting them directly, physically, and visually as if they were taking their place among the objects and events of real life; as if, as the name implies, magic were an everyday phenomenon.

The new American theater has now begun to recognize this technique as a potent tool to expand the expressive resources of the drama. It has two immensely attractive advantages. One is that it does not require American actors to abandon their excellent training in psychological portrayal (as for instance the minimalist theater, the Brechtian theater, allegorical theater, and the "stage picture" method all must do to some extent). The other is that it seems to be genuinely popular with the public. Marquez's novel *One Hundred Years of Solitude* and Borges's *Ficciones* were international bestsellers, and the theatrical use of magic realism—perhaps Schaffer's *Equus* is an example—offers an audience spectacle and magic without abandoning the interest of charater and psychology, and without excessive demands on its hermeneutical resources.

Most important of all, magic realism on stage does not in any way detract from the storytelling function of theater. Indeed, story is enriched and intensified, as in a fairy tale; and a space is opened for the natural entry of the great myths and archetypes of our collective human dream. In another sense theater can begin once more to function as ritual, as shamanic passage into the spirit world.

The Tempest is again almost the ideal vehicle for this new kind of exploration of theater. It is a play of and about magic, and its greatest lines celebrate the fact that we are such stuff as dreams are made on. Though at the end of the play Prospero abjures his rough magic, it has done its work. The magic of

theater, Hirsch told me, is there to teach, cure, and transform.
And this is perhaps why I was so deeply moved by Curchack's
performance of the play. The actor made appear the very stuff
of one's dream life, and thus enabled one to claim its beauties
and its powers, as well as its terrors, for one's own. Julie
Taymor's production reportedly did the same thing, realizing
and externalizing the inner world.

THE PHILOSOPHICAL THEATER

Behind the current crop of *Tempests* loom three very influential
less recent productions of it: John Hirsch's at the Mark Taper
in 1979; Liviu Ciulei's dark, strange, and philosophical staging
at the Guthrie in 1980, with Prospero's cell an atelier surrounded by a moat of blood filled with the detritus of western
civilization; and Giorgio Strehler's gigantic operatic version of
it in Milan in 1983. What these productions did was to give
permission, so to speak, for a theater that would be free to
explore the deepest and most ancient ideas and values: a return
to a theater of meaning. They set the play against the immense
backdrop of nature, of history, of the physical universe, of the
myths of humankind. Without putting words in the mouths of
any individual performer or director, let me sketch out the
main themes of what I take to be the new intellectual predicament in the American theater, as it shows up in *The Tempest*.

The play has become a kind of marker, indicating the end of
one age and the difficult birth of another. The core of
modernism was a moral, political, and esthetic theory of indis-
criminate rebellion against authority, bourgeois values, and
traditional modes of culture and thought; it has inspired artists
since the French Revolution. But this intellectual movement is
now increasingly bankrupt. We have seen art in the service of
revolutionary ideology, utopian political theory, and the socialist State, and it does not smell very good. Our heroes are
increasingly those who resist that attempt to strip us of our
history, and who stand in solidarity with the traditional values
of human beings.

Late modernism, in its desperation for original modes of
rebellion and iconoclasm, had celebrated violence, cruelty,
sexual perversity, and self-destruction; "performance artists"
had mutilated their very bodies in the frenzy to escape how
things are and demonstrate their rejection of the world. Likewise they had begun to attack and erode the fundamental

forms of their art itself: story, language, fiction, stage set, personality, performer, performance, rehearsal, and audience— like a ship that tears up its own planking to feed its furnace. Meanwhile artists had, largely by their own fault, alienated and exiled themselves from the real world and from their public. This process had to stop somewhere; and what we have seen is either the appearance of a new avant-garde, much more in touch with the shared and ancient values of humanity, or the disappearance of the avant-garde as a guarantee of the seriousness of art altogether.

Part of this change is a matter of demographics. The young turks are now in charge, and have the responsibility of guiding their culture. Mark Lamos told me ruefully that his own experience of being an artistic director, of being the one to give orders, the tree in which the birds make their nest, so to speak, had fed his interpretation of *The Tempest,* which among other things is about authority, the rightfulness of authority, and the renunciation of it. The play concerns a traditional ruler who brings about a counterrevolution against the tyranny that overthrew his government, and who puts down the revolutionaries and is restored to his legitimate position of rule. Likewise, it portrays an artist—Shakespeare's own word for Prospero— who returns from exile to take up his rightful place in society.

The play deals also with the other side of authority, with those who serve, those over whom authority is rightly or wrongly exercised, and with the issues of bondage and liberation. This topic has been part of the bad conscience of the West, but it cannot be repressed forever. The play gives us a way of beginning to examine the issue philosophically. Almost all the current productions of the play are deeply ambivalent about Caliban: on the one hand he is the dispossessed third world colonial subject or slave, arousing all of the old revolutionary sympathies; but on the other he is a rapist, a brutal male who cannot be cultivated into gentleness and self-control and who must therefore be governed by magical force.

The Tempest contains a gentle and sympathetic rebuttal of all those utopian and ahistorical political ideas whose results have been so bloody in our century; gentle and sympathetic, because the primitive communism of Montaigne's cannibals, which would eventually inspire the revolutionaries Rousseau and Marx, is put in the mouth of good old Gonzalo and denied by the cynics Sebastian and Antonio. But the rebuttal is final and undeniable: the only way Gonzalo could bring about the withering away of the state would be to be the absolute ruler of it. On the other hand *The Tempest* is by no means a conservative play. After all, Prospero does voluntarily divest himself of colonial power, and, having liberated the island's inhabitants, restores it to its original possessors. It is no wonder that, after Vietnam, Grenada, and the Philippines, the play might be deeply interesting to American directors.

The emphasis has changed from the political or moral activist to the creative artist (or scientist), and this change is reflected in the dominance of Prospero over the Italian conspirators. Likewise, the center of interest has shifted from the young lovers rebelling against parental authority to the parent himself, who, ironically, forbids their love only to test, refine, and strengthen it. Authorship and authority are related, and creativity more often involves patient construction and nurture than rebellion. The nature of the creative imagination itself is at the center of this play, and in the recent productions of it Ariel, the symbol of that imagination, is almost always the most attractive and spectacular figure.

In many productions of the play the scientific and technological sources of civilized power are reassessed, brought back within the purview of artistic and humane consideration, and grafted back to the ancient ritual and magical roots of human culture. In the nineteenth and early twentieth centuries, it might well have seemed that science and technology were the enemies of art and deserved their banishment thence. But in the new science of the late twentieth century, theoretical physics can find common ground with oriental mysticism; free, self-organizing systems are quite plausible not only in the human world but throughout the world of matter; our common inheritance with the higher animals has become for us a source of strength and health, not a restriction on our freedom; and our human creativity now appears to be only the intensest form of the generous creativity of nature. Meanwhile we have begun to see how a more sophisticated technology can act in harmony with nature and even begin to heal the scars that our earlier and cruder technologies have bequeathed us.

In many contemporary productions of *The Tempest,* Prospero's role as renaissance scientist is emphasized and reassessed. Robert Falls told me that there was an intellectual continuity between his recent *Galileo,* his *Sunday in the Park with George,* and his *Tempest.* The artist, the scientist, and the magician shared a common predicament and a common destiny. Woodruff's set included a blackboard covered with scientific formulae and diagrams, and had in the background containers of uranium and oil. Scientific and technological motifs were present also in the versions of Curchack, Ciulei, Hirsch, and Breuer. Curchack does wonderful things with fire, the traditional promethean symbol of *techne*. Theatrically, this thing of darkness—science—we are now acknowledging to be our own. And this play, in which Shakespeare tackles the whole problem of science and art, and makes prophetic pronouncements on it, is an ideal vehicle for this acknowledgement.

The Tempest is an outcropping of that great modern myth of the wizard/scientist, his voluntary unmasking, his beautiful daughter, the transcendence and incorporation of the beast-man and the wicked witch, the test of worthiness, and the initiation of and handing over of power to a younger generation, which we find in Mozart's *The Magic Flute* and in the film version of *The Wizard of Oz*. The myth is a reply to the Faust/Frankenstein myth, which warns us against the acquisition of forbidden knowledge and power; it shows us how that knowledge and power can be morally tested and found to be in accord with nature and with justice. Deepest of all, it is a replaying of the myth of Eden and the Fall, and a renegotiation of the human contract that was first made there, only on better terms. Conscious and unconscious references to these other versions of the myth can be found throughout the performances of *The Tempest* that I have seen. "Pay no attention to the man behind the curtain," says the Wizard to Dorothy; but the unveiling of authority, and the passing it along so that each person can become his or her own, is at the core. *The Tempest* awards us all a heart, a medal of valor, a Doctorate of Thinkology, if we are willing to take them on; and the magic flute, scarlet slippers, or magician's cloak by which it is accomplished signify the traditional genres of performing art, now augmented by new technological power and natural scientific knowledge.

A NEW ECOLOGICAL ETHICS

The next section, on ecology, begins by proposing a third way of thinking about the land, between the conventional opposites of the raped and exploited wasteland and the protected virgin wilderness: that is, the fertile and culti-vated garden in which human beings have a creative part to play in the evolution and improvement of nature.

This garden ethic is explored in a close discussion of prairie restoration, which is seen both as the heir to the ancient European tradition of the Arcadian landscape, and also as a promise of a future in which human beings will seed earthly forms of life upon other planets, and transform them in turn into living worlds where human beings can live in the open air.

4   Cultivating the American Garden

Suppose the Grand Canyon were man-made. It could have been formed (though it wasn't) by agricultural or industrial erosion; the results of poor farming methods can look very similar—artificial badlands—if on a smaller scale. Would this hideous scar on the fair face of the earth still be a national park? Would anyone visit it other than groups of awed school-children studying Environmental Destruction, absorbing the dreadful lesson of what can happen to a desert raped by human exploiters? Strip mining can produce spectacular and dramatic landscapes. W. H. Auden loved the lead-mining landscape of Cornwall above all others; the evocative and aromatic hillsides of the Mediterranean, with their olives, sages, thyme, and dwarf conifers, are a result of centuries of deforestation, goat herding, and the building of navies, roads, and cities. The Niagara Falls may one day have to be shored up to make them look "natural"; for they are eating their way back an inch a year and will "naturally" dwindle into ordinary rapids. To an ecologist unschooled in American myth, the most aston-ishingly unnatural places on earth would be certain regions of the American continent from which the presence of the domi-nant species—us—had ben meticulously removed, as if a million acres had been cleared of earthworms. I mean, of course, the wilderness areas.

The cognitive dissonances that many Americans may have experienced while reading this first paragraph suggest a prob-lem in our use of the words "nature" and "natural." If we define natural as that which is opposed to human, then we must face the fact that we are "scientific" creationists and should be on the side of those who would have the school boards ban even the mention of evolution. If we define natural as that which is opposed to social and cultural, while insisting that humans are natural, then we will have revealed our adherence to a theory of human nature (Rousseau's, actually) asserting that humankind is naturally solitary and unsocial, a theory that all of the human sciences—anthropology, psychology, paleoanthropology, linguistics, ethology—emphatically deny. But if everything that happens is natural, including Love Canal and Alamogordo, then what becomes of our tendency to value the natural and revere nature? And if the word refers to everything, is it of any use at all?

All societies, Lévi-Strauss tells us, distinguish between culture and nature. But the philosophical, moral, and esthetic dimensions of the distinction differ profoundly from one society to another. Indeed, one might almost categorize societies, in a way that would nicely cut across the usual economic, technological, and historical distinctions, solely by the content of their nature/culture distinction. Is nature "good" and culture "bad," or vice versa? Is nature dynamic and culture static, or the other way around? Is nature self-aware and culture innocent? Is nature personal, culture collective? Is it important for a society to emphasize the distinction in some of these categories, while denying it in others? Do not the factional, ideological, and political conflicts within all cultures consist to a larg extent in a struggle over the strategic definition of these words and their exclusive possession?

Each of us surely has a pretty good idea of the "correct" answers to these questions of definition; where and how do we learn them? Are we prepared to argue for them? If someone else's answers are different from mine, is she wrong? Tasteless? Wicked?

There is a wonderful exchange on this problem of definition in Shakespeare's *The Winter's Tale*. Perdita has just declared that she won't have carnations or "streak'd gillyvors" in her garden because, like an American nature freak, she disapproves of the fact that they have been bred and hybridized by genetic technology.

Perdita. ...There is an art, which in their piedness shares
With great creating Nature.

Polixenes.   Say there be;
Yet Nature is made better by no mean
But Nature makes that mean; so, o'er that art,
Which you say adds to Nature, is an art
That Nature makes. You see, sweet maid, we marry
A gentler scion to the wildest stock,

And make conceive a bark of baser kind
By bud of nobler race. This is an art
Which does mend Nature, change it rather; but
The art itself is Nature.

As usual, Shakespeare says it all: the subtext here is that Perdita is a base shepherdess who wants to marry the prince, Polixenes' son; but of course, she is really a princess herself, though she doesn't know it. Without going into the complexities of lineage, breeding, and social convention that are at work here, let us look at what this passage tells us about gardening. First of all, Shakespeare has clearly grasped the distinction between mere growth and what came to be called evolution. Aristotle amended Plato's system, in which all change was essentially pathological and incoherent, by proposing the notion of a foreordained and meaningful growth proper to each individual species. However, the idea of that radical evolutionary change by which one species turns into another would have been nauseating to him. Shakespeare's Perdita has already observed what Darwin noticed 200 years later, that changes in species can be brought about by selective breeding and hybridization—those primitive forms of recombinant DNA bioengineering. She doesn't like it, but Shakespeare gives Polixenes a remarkable argument in favor of human tampering with the essence of life itself. He takes up Perdita's snide use of the word "art" and turns it around to include perhaps even the very dramatic medium in which he has his being. He insists that human art is not only a product of nature, but one of the creative instruments of nature in doing what it does. *We* are *natura naturans,* nature naturing.

Most of us, asked what nature is, would probably make a vague gesture toward the nearest patch of green vegetation and say, to begin with, something like "Well, it's what's out there, not what's in here." A little prompting would elicit any number of other imaginary characteristics; one can go out into nature, but even when one is in it, it is still "out there." Nature was here before we (the colonists and immigrants) came, and in fact was here before the Indians. Nature bears the weight of our activities, but in the long run renews itself and remains just as it was. Left to itself, nature settles into a balance, a rhythm, that is eternal and unchanging. (Do we not recognize the phrases from countless Walt Disney wildlife movies?) Nature is dangerous but purifying, innocent yet wise, the only real touchstone of what is good and right and beautiful.

It should be clear that this nature has very little in common with natural reality as it is illuminated for us by science. Nature, according to science, is as much "in here" as it is "out there." Our bodies and brains are a result of evolution, which is a natural process so paradigmatic that it could almost be said to be synomymous with nature itself. Moreover, we are by nature social, having been naturally selected, through millions of years of overlapping genetic and cultural evolution, to live in a cooperative cultural matrix. The most powerful selective pressure on our genes since our line broke away from those of the other primates has prompted us toward cities; thus we are by nature hairless, brainy, infantile, gregarious, oversexed, long-lived, artistic, talkative, and religious.

If we want to fall back on saying that the natural is what has not been interfered with, as opposed, say, to the artificial, science will give us little comfort. For a scientists who must take observable and measurable evidence as the only warrant for the reality of being, the universe is exactly and only the interference of everything with everything else. Quantum theory shows that nothing can be observed or measured without being interfered with; if nature is what has not been interfered with, nature does not exist.

Nature, as revealed by evolutionary biology, paleobiology, and geology, is violent, unbalanced, improvisatory, dynamic. The new paradigm in paleobiology, as it is expounded in the symposium, *Earth's Earliest Biosphere: Its Origin and Evolution,* under the editorship of J. William Schopf, holds that the first living inhabitants of the planet, whose metabolisms were anaerobic, so thoroughly poisoned their own ecosphere that they were forced to develop protective mechanisms or to retreat to marginal ecological niches. Indeed, the poison gas with which they polluted the atmosphere was the corrosive element oxygen. Luckily, new life-forms evolved that were able to use the explosive powers of oxygen as a source of energy, and they went on to develop eukaryotic cell structure, multicellular organization, sex, and eventually us.

It is worth quoting the sober prose of some of the contributors to the symposium. J. M. Hayes: "An environment without oxygen, the earth was then a different planet...the paleobiological record shows, nevertheless, that life existed on that different planet, and it is widely held that the advent of oxygenic photosynthesis [the release of oxygen as a byproduct of living metabolism using light as an energy source, as modern plants do] was the singular event that led eventually to our modern environment." David J. Chapman and J. William Schopf: "The toxicity of uncombined oxygen is well-established. ...Obviously, therefore the appearance of oxygen-producing photosynthesis and a resulting oxygenic environment necessitated the development of a series of intracellular protective devices and scavengers, particularly in those organisms producing oxygen and in those nonmobile organisms that were unable to use behavioral mechanisms to escape the effects of this newly abundant reactive gas."

Our precious oxygen, then, is the toxic waste of the first polluters. Imagine the cataclysm this must have been for those early life-forms: for millions of years, the poison advanced and retreated, leaving an extraordinary record of its vicissitudes in iron-banded rock formations, which show alternate layers of rusted (oxidized) and unrusted (unoxidized) iron ore. But the pollution won in the end; and the "natural" species of the time were replaced by what our authors call "a new, highly successful mode of evolutionary advance, one based chiefly on the development of new morphologies and innovative body plans among megascopic, multicellular, sexually reproducing eukaryotes."

It does not get us off the hook to define nature as the unreflexive, the unpremeditated, and thus distinguish it from human cultural activity. Obviously, it would be foolish to impute human values and motives to natural phenomena other than ourselves. But it would be even more foolish to assert uniqueness in the possession of motives and values. It would clearly be wrong to deny that a raccoon can see because it doesn't have the same sort of brain as we do. It would be just as wrong to deny to the raccoon the calculating, and in some sense self-aware, intentions that its every move with relation to the garbage can announces. And when one studies the responses of a whole species' gene pool to environmental change—responses which seem powerfully to imply anticipation and preparation for future changes—one comes to feel that the rest of nature is no more innocent than we. Our cunning and reflexiveness are simply faster than anything else's. Nature's specialty is reflexiveness, and we are better at it than the rest of nature. The DNA molecule is the reflexiveness of matter; the animal mind is the reflexiveness of instinct; the human mind is the reflexiveness of the animal mind.

Nature is the process of increasing self-reference and self-measurement. Evolution is how nature finds out what it is. In the first moment of the Big Bang it didn't have the faintest idea. It didn't even have laws to obey. It lucked into the first ones, and has been improvising in the direction of greater definiteness and concreteness ever since. We human beings are what nature has provisionally defined itself as being, given the richest field of permutations (terrestrial chemistry) and the longest period of unhindered research; indeed, there may well be a scientific sense in which "the proper study of mankind is man."

But if nature is not innocent, perhaps it can still be wise. Alas, no again. Those of us who have seen an incompetent squirrel miss the easy branch he was aiming at, or have reflected more gloomily on the idiotic and improvident proliferation of relatively simple and inflexible biomes (climax forests, for instance), must suspect that nature in general is at least as capable of making mistakes as the representative of it that is most embarrassed by its own mistakes: ourselves.

On the other hand, nature is pathetically willing, as it were. The flowers growing in the desolation of Mount St. Helens testify to what in human beings we would call a lunatic hopefulness, the optimism of the amateur. Or consider the courtship ritual of the blue satin bowerbird, which, convinced that its own color is the most beautiful in the world, builds the bluest nest it can to attract its mate, painting it with chewed-up blueberries and decorating it with blue flowers, bits of blue paper, and its own feathers; a nest which, since it is on the ground and vulnerable to predators, is never used by the lucky bride. (She later builds a sensible little nest in a tree.) This charming unwisdom is more attractive, perhaps, than wisdom. Wisdom sits still and doesn't make a fool of itself. Nature sends in the clowns.

If our prejudices about nature can be so wrong, perhaps we are just as wrong about its antonym, culture. For Americans, culture means to a large extent technology; indeed, the latter might well be named more frequently as the opposite of nature. If nature, in our myth, is eternal, unchanging, pure, gentle, wise, innocent, balanced, harmonious, and good, then culture (*qua* technology) must be temporary, progressive, polluting, violent, blind, sophisticated, distorted, destructive, and evil. At its best, technology is for us an euphoric escape from nature; at its worst, a diabolical destruction of it. Our "gut" meaning for technology is machines of metal, oil, and electricity; we often forget that technology, strictly speaking, also includes the violins of Stradivarius, horsebreeding, handwriting, yeast baking, orchards, cheesemaking, and villanelles.

This ideological opposition of culture and nature—with no mediating term—has had real consequences. More often than need be, Americans confronted with a natural landscape have either exploited it or designated it a wilderness area. The polluter and the ecology freak are two faces of the same coin; they both perpetuate a theory about nature that allows no alternative to raping it or tying it up in a plastic bag to protect it from contamination.

How did we come to this peculiar view of nature and culture? The two great historical givens in American culture are Puritanism and the frontier. The defining characteristic of Puritanism is its denial of the validity and permissibility of mediating terms. Puritanism abhors the corruptions of ritual and mystery. It insists upon an absolute sincerity untainted by practical or esthetic considerations; it has promoted a view of marriage in which any compromise with family and property interests is a base betrayal of the spiritual absolute of love; and, as is clear in the works of Nathaniel Hawthorne, it has a horror of any spiritual miscegenation between the human and the natural. Like the small boy who will eat only food whose living origin has been utterly pummeled out of it, the Puritan likes his nature as spiritually dead as a doornail.

The frontier experience both confirmed and profoundly modified this predisposition. In the first place, the frontier seemed to be the embodiment of the boundary between matter and spirit. Matter was "out there" beyond the frontier; spirit was "in here" among the brethren; and the witch-hunt preserved the distinction. But the Puritan distrust of the means of expression and of the accommodations and compromises that make society possible led to a revulsion of feeling that we find raised to noble eloquence and genuine insight in the works of Thoreau. The true assertion of the purity of the spirit was to "go back to nature," to build a cabin in the woods, to ship aboard a whaler, to be a mountain man, to "light out for the Territory," as Huck Finn puts it, and leave behind the soft, corrupting, and emasculating sophistications of "sivilization." In nature one could discover for oneself the real meaning of America's political liberation: our natural solitude, our natural equality, our natural selfishness. From this myth has come great good and

great evil: the realized ideal of huge populations living in freedom from the ancient and degrading limitations of conservative
technologies, as well as the heroic glory of the space program
—but also the daily abandonment of wives by their husbands
and the odd ethics of defaulting on child support.

If nature is the opposite of society, then the natural man is
essentially asocial, or even antisocial. So Rousseau argued, at
any rate, and though the idea has done more damage in France
than in America, it has been very influential on this side of
the Atlantic. To its credit, it has been used to justify the sturdy
individualism enshrined in the Constitution; we vote one by
one in the privacy of a booth, and this solitary act is at the
core of our political system. Likewise, we vote by our choice of
purchase in the free market, and our instinctual bias for the
individual helps defend the market against the pressures of
monopoly capitalism, paternalistic government, restrictive
trade unions, and puritanical consumer groups. If the most
important human unit is the individual, then the courts should
rule in favor of the individual in every case where he or she
comes into conflict with other human units (the family, the
neighborhood, the corporate body).

As an empirical fact, our natural solitude has little scientific
foundation. We evolved as social beings; our ancestors were
tribal; our babies cannot grow up without the company of their
kind, and so an *enfant sauvage,* that ancient human dream of
innocence, would be impossible; our closest relatives, the
chimpanzees and gorillas, are so social that it has been said
that "one chimpanzee is no chimpanzees." The notion of
natural solitude has thus introduced distortions into what
might otherwise have been a more harmonious balance of con-
stitutional guarantees. Those distortions include the neglect
and isolation of persons, especially the young and old; we
regard privacy as a natural right, but not community, which
may well be a more important human need. As the Talking
Heads have said of "people like us," we don't want freedom,
we don't want justice, we just want someone to love.

The notion of natural equality has been brought to the rescue
of that grand old phrase in the Declaration of Independence:
"We hold these truths to be self-evident; that all men are created
equal." This phrase appears to be an empirical statement about
human nature and as such is buttressed by the authority of
Plato, Hobbes, and Rousseau. But suppose it were simply
wrong? There is virtual unanimity among the human sciences

that great variations in natural abilities exist among human beings. Indeed, a social species based on the cooperative division of labor cannot survive without variation in natural capacities. Is it not therefore unwise to hold the Constitution hostage to an erroneous claim that equality is an empirical fact? The wording of this phrase (we "hold" these truths to be truths) suggests a wiser alternative: that equality is something we stipulate as a ground rule, perhaps as a corrective to our natural inequality.

Other distortions have been created by the notion of natural self-interest. Modern sociobiology, anthropology, and psychology show that self-interest is not the fundamental human drive but only one of several, which include deeply instinctive impulses toward altruism, sacrifice, agonistic behavior, gregariousness, and loyalty. The entirely self-interested individual is clearly a grotesque pathological aberration produced by extraordinary circumstances, the exception that proves the rule. Perhaps those circumstances might be reproduced if the impersonal state or corporation were totally to supplant the community (which is what Pol Pot, no doubt a devoted student of Rousseau during his years in Paris, was trying to do in Cambodia), but the last few years have shown how durable, indeed how unexpectedly flourishing, are the ethnic, religious, and microcultural communities in the heart of the modern world.

Do the Europeans handle the nature/culture distinction any better than we? In some sense, yes. The greatest moments of European cultural brilliance have overcome the falseness and the sterility of the distinction: the gardens of Hadrian, of the Medicis, of the Bourbons, of the great English gardeners. Perhaps the Republic itself. The Renaissance city. The lovers in Shakespeare and Mozart. French and Italian cuisine. The bourgeois family, that vitally creative—if flawed—institution. Claude Lorrain and Nicholas Poussin and Claude Monet. Baroque music. Gardens, music, landscape painting, cooking: each mediates between culture and nature in a fertile and inventive way.

But the Europeans have run up against the limits of their own ideas. For Europe, freedom is a choice between alternatives that are finally limited. Culture and nature may be in greater harmony, but they are both constrained by a system that is entropically running down. For Americans, true freedom is not the choice at the ballot box but the opportunity to create a new world out of nothing: a Beverly Hills, a Disneyland, a Dallas, a Tranquility Base. Growth can still happen in Europe, but evolution will happen in America, if its academic discouragers do not prevail—and it will take place in the personal as well as the cosmic sphere.

The European model of kinship is parental: we are defined by where and whom we came from, and the cause, the parent, is more full of that quality that characterizes the effect than is the effect itself. Only if the child can transcend the parent, and if the parent measures her own success solely by the transcendence, can evolution take place in the cultural realm. Americans model kinship not on parenthood but on marriage; not on the relationship we are given but on the relationship we create. So the child can be grater than the parent, the effect more essential than the cause, the creation more creative than the creator; even eternity, as Blake (a natural American) put it, is in love with the productions of time. The European past is a prison; the American past is the most wonderful raw material. The European future is "held in store," as they say; but the American futures are to be created.

We do not need to accept our myth of nature and culture. The state of America is the state of being able to change our myths. We can forge in the smithies of our souls the conscience of our race, a project James Joyce gave up as impossible for Ireland. Thoreau rejoiced in the indubitable capacity to change himself by conscious endeavor; the wood of Melville's ship of human destiny "could only be American."

But Thoreau and Melville still bear the marks of damage by the American myth; both needed to escape the complications of heterosexual relationships and go back to nature, to achieve what they achieved. Henry James and T. S. Eliot had to move to England to begin to garden their impressions. Contemporary women writers must likewise dismiss the male culture to find a space to breathe, and must likewise suffer an impoverishment of that "radiant and porous" creativity which Virginia Woolf rightly located in androgyny. So, then: How do we change our myth? What model do we use to heal the breach in our ideas and to release the enormous cultural energies of a new American renaissance?

I believe that we must trust human intention more than human instinct, because intention evolved out of and as an improvement upon instinct. But if intention is to be thus trusted, it must be fully instructed in the instincts that are its springboard and raw material; otherwise, intention may do more harm than good. For this instruction, we must turn not only to the human sciences but also to the species' ancient wisdom as it is preserved in myths, rituals, fairy tales, and the traditions of the performing arts. Perhaps our soundest model will be the art of gardening.

We know that we can ruin things, especially complex and subtle things, by that domineering overconsciousness that Coleridge saw in himself as "the intellect that kills" and that Keats diagnosed in him as an "irritable grasping after fact and reason." Shakespeare implies in *The Winter's Tale* that the human power of transformation need not be like that at all. To create, to use our technology—our "art," as he calls it— is as natural to us as breathing, if we do it the right way. Let us accept our self-consciousness as appropriate to us, and rejoice in its occasional absurdity, rather than attempt to escape into a kind of prelapsarian spontaneity. Our spontaneity must be found at the heart of our self-awareness, and nowhere else. It is not enough to be, as Coleridge put it, "wisely passive" before nature; we know from quantum theory that reality reveals itself only to the active questioner. And if acting is natural to us, then we may achieve in action a contemplative absorption that is as wise as any meditative trance.

Any gardener will instantly recognize the state of mind I have just described. As one moves about the flower beds, weeding, propagating, pruning the apple tree, shifting the rock in the rock garden an inch or two to make room for the roots of a healthy erica, one becomes a subtle and powerful force of natural selection in that place, placing one's stamp on the future of the biosphere; but it feels like pottering, like a waking dream. "Meantime the mind, from pleasure less/Withdraws into its happiness," says Marvell.

The creation and use of other technologies, even those of steel and glass and oil and electricity, need be no different. It is all gardening, if we see it right. If we distrust our technology, we distrust our own nature, and nature itself. And this distrust inevitably makes us helpless and passive before the technical powers of others, and resentful, and disenfranchised. Let us seize our powers to ourselves: our artistic and esthetic capacities, which make use of the whole brain, not just the anxious calculatons of the linguistic centers in the left temporal lobe.

We must take responsibility for nature. That ecological

modesty which asserts that we are only one species among many, with no special rights, we may now see as the abdication of a trust. We are, whether we like it or not, the lords of creation; true humility consists not in pretending that we aren't, but in living up to the trust that it implies by service to the greater glory and beauty of the world we have been given to look after. It is a bad shepherd who, on democratic principles, deserts his sheep.

The time is ripe to begin planting the American garden. This demands an assessment of such cultural resources as already exist. America has access not only to the great European traditions of gardening but also to the glorious legacies of the Chinese, the Japanese, and the Indians. One large and unique role that the American garden can fulfill is that of synthesis, the harmonious and fertile juxtaposition of past and foreign cultures. But is there not something of its own that America can contribute to the tradition?

On the face of it, the project of an American garden may not look promising. In the vernacular, the word "garden" has come to mean little better than a vegetable patch; its substitutes, "yard" and "lawn," seem explicitly to deny an artistic or decorative intent. Nevertheless, our garden can draw on the unique promise of American developments in the great mediators between nature and culture: cookery, music, and the family. Cookery transforms raw nature into the substance of human communion, routinely and without fuss transubstantiating matter into mind; in the past twenty years, American cuisine has been transformed from something resembling British or German provincial cooking into a serious and sophisticated art with virtuoso practitioners and a solid literature. Music, as Bosch knew, is at once the most sensual of pleasures and the loftiest and most divine exercise of the spirit; because it doesn't seem to depend on ideas, music has never embarrassed the American genius, and our domestic amalgam of jazz, bluegrass, European folk and art music, and the blues is now the classical idiom of the entire world. As for the American family, its special promise has already been pointed out: our emphasis on the elective aspects of the family puts the human intention of the spouses themselves in charge of family life in a way that is unprecedented among human societies. If the gardening of a marriage becomes imaginatively feasible, we will have a chance at a remarkable psychic enfranchisement for parents and children alike.

The American garden will not just be what George Steiner calls an "archive of Eden": a collection of good ideas from elsewhere. Such a vision of America derives from the suicidal European notion that we are at the end of history, with nothing left to us but a cataloguing of the past or a suitably tasteful self-annihilation. But if we are to avoid being merely derivative, we must be bold in our assessment of the raw materials of the American garden, and reject nothing until it has fully proved its uselessness—not even Disneyland, the shopping malls of the Sunbelt, the atriums of Hyatt hotels, the imaginary Ringworld gardens of the High Frontier, their lakes and forests vertiginously slathered over the inner surface of a gigantic aluminum band spinning in the cloudless dazzle of the naked sun. Let us consider the sheer scale of America, and the perspective of it as seen from the freeway, the Ferris wheel, the skyscraper, the jet plane. There is enough room to plant gardens for all the citizens of the republic, not just a wealthy aristocracy. Let us make a virtue of the colossal earthworks we have dug for our industrial purposes, and of our capacity for truly heroic alterations of the landscape.

This American garden will not only grow, but evolve; and that means it must encompass change and death and self-awareness (which is the awareness of death). This is why water, which flows, shatters itself, and reflects, is so important in a garden. The true artists of Eden have always built into it a sort of shiver, the possibility of a cloud passing over the sun and transforming the glowing landscape into a tragic or heroic mode. Coleridge's Xanadu has its terrifying chasm, its caverns measureless to man, its sunless sea. "Is there no change of death in paradise?" asks Wallace Stevens, and answers: "Death is the mother of beauty." He is echoing that artist who painted a skull in his pastoral landscape and inscribed next to it, in a mossy stone, the words *et in Arcadia ego:* yes, I too am in Arcadia.

5   *Restoring the American Prairie*

At first it looks like a big untidy field—tall grass infested with weeds. But then looking a little longer and a little more carefully, the eye reorders it. There is an unfamiliar, breathtaking pale-yellowish jade freshness in the green, a preciseness and laciness in the texture that remind you of the wildflowers of rocky seacoasts or alpine meadows. Then you realize that all of those plants are *supposed* to be there, and if you know the species you recognize the towering bluestem and indian grass in the damper hollows, the twisted awns of the drier stipa, the feathery offset florets of the side oats grama, the brilliant emerald clumps of hair-leaved dropseed.

Then there are the forbs, the broadleaved plants. Some are giants: the compassplant, with its leathery handlike leaves, turned edge-on to the sun at its height to conserve moisture; the blanched ultraviolet flowers of the downy phlox; the black-eyed susan, the hoary puccoon and the coneflower; and below, the cold green shields of the prairie dock, the exquisite turk's head lily, the leadplant thought by early miners to indicate the presence of ore, the wild indigo, the tiny lobelia, the purple and white prairie clovers; and look, a mottled white-violet-chocolate prairie orchid.

On the drier slopes that heave up sunlit into a sky darkening toward a squall, you can see wild roses, sage, horsetails, euphorbias; and there are seedlings from the nearby grove of savanna oaks that will, if a prairie fire does not kill them, transform these grassy hills after a few decades into a shadowy forest. A yellow butterfly staggers against the clouds; deer turn and move away into the trees.

This *is* a prairie, then; no doubt about it. You breathe that American sigh of relief that says that you have made a clean getaway, found a place to settle, build a hogan, light a fire, raise some kids. Back to nature; at home on the range.

But again things are not always as they seem. This is Greene Prairie, planted forty years ago by the ecological restorationist Henry Greene on forty acres of degraded Wisconsin farmland, as part of the University of Wisconsin's arboretum at Madison. Almost every prairie plant here is descended from seeds or whole specimens found in old cemeteries, along railroad right-of-way, or other unfarmed scraps of land.

How does one plant a prairie? First the existing vegetation—mostly European grasses or pantropic weeds—must be burnt off. Bulldozers dig ponds to allow alien material to settle out. The height of the water table is taken into account. Sweating gangs of young men and women in dungarees (volunteers today; in the thirties, when the earliest prairies were started, the workers were paid a living wage by the WPA) harvest the wild seeds or dig up clumps of virgin sod. A prairie contains over two hundred species of plants alone, not counting the bacteria, the mycorrhizal fungi in the rootweb, the insects, animals, and birds. The land is planted; then the real hard work, the weeding, begins. The volunteers must be drilled meticulously on the differences between native and alien species; the whole affair resembles a ritual, complete with ecologist-shamans, adepts, novices, ordeals, and mystical instruction. This procedure engenders an extraordinary familiarity with the land. I have seen Keith Wendt, an ecologist who had worked at the arboretum but had been away from it for several years, walk straight across the prairie to a single tiny flower that he wanted to point out to me. It was a very rare species, and he knew exactly where it was.

After a few seasons of backbreaking work the prairie is established and, as if it were a single organism, it begins to police and nourish itself. Much has been written on the marvelous interdependence of species in the wild; the most recent thinking treats such ecological systems as if they were indeed single entities, with different organs for different functions. The Gaia Hypothesis, advanced by the visionary British ecologist James Lovelock, proposes that the planet itself is such an organism, a living unity in the wastes of space. In the prairie the fine network of mycorrhizal fungi which flourishes below the soil surface acts as a primitive nervous system, linking the plants and regulating the flow of nutrients. The actual soil of a healthy prairie is paradoxically very poor, because almost all of the nutrients are in circulation in the living biomass. To make a prairie fertile, you must kill it.

When one has planted one's prairie, what exactly has one got?

In the previous essay, I called for an American garden, a new tradition that would bridge the deep and damaging gap in the American imagination between nature and humanity, the protected wilderness area and the exploited landscape. I came to the Wisconsin Arboretum in search of that garden, and I believe that I found it—or at least one of the core elements of it—in the work of the ecological restorationists.

It seems to me that we have here the philosophical elements of a new kind of environmental ethic, one that accepts human participation as essential to the wholeness of the world, and that actively seeks out ways in which that participation can be deepened and extended. It could be argued that the lovely complex tissue of the biosphere, threatened as it is, needs our best talents if it is to survive.

We may find our greatest hopes for the future, as did the Renaissance itself, in a re-creation of the past; the prairie may be the best long-term rotation crop for farm areas suffering from soil erosion and impoverishment. This vision is Arcadian in the best sense. If the restored prairie is one prototype of the American garden, that garden is the culmination of the Arcadian tradition.

What is Arcadia? One may find it in the paintings of Giorgione, Bellini, Titian, of Lorrain, Poussin, Chardin. In the western landscape gardening tradition it consists of a set of tastes handed down from the biblical gardens of Egypt and Babylon, through the Greek gardens celebrated by Homer in his mythical Phaiakia, to the Roman gardens of volcanic Sicily, Naples, and the Alban hills; and thence to the gardens of northern Europe—Pope's Twickenham garden, Stourhead, Monet's Clos Normand at Giverny, Hidcote, Sissinghurst; and then across the Atlantic to the painted landscapes of the Hudson School, the literary ones of Thoreau, and the real ones of Frederick Law Olmsted. There is a happy return to European models in the glorious American gardens of Longwood and Dumbarton Oaks. It took the bitter check of the Dust Bowl to bring about the last, severest, and most demanding realization of the Arcadian ideal. That realization first appeared in the imagination of Aldo Leopold, the author of *Sand County Almanac,* one of the founders of the University of Wisconsin Arboretum and the father of its restored prairie.

Arcadia, if we may characterize it generically, is a place

where human beings cooperate with nature to produce a richness of ecological variety that would not otherwise exist. It
undergoes continuous mild change, and is very adaptable to
minor ecological alteration; but at the same time it is conservative and preserves things as they were in the Golden Age.
Perhaps it is a country of the mind only, but we can see traces
of it in the hills of Tuscany, the hedgerow and beech landscape
of the Cotswolds, the savannas of Africa, and the prairies of
the midwest.

We human beings have a natural tropism towards such
places, perhaps because they remind us in some genetic way of
the savannas where we achieved our definitive evolution as
the species we are. Our names for it—"Paradise," which means
a royal hunting-park; "The Happy Hunting Grounds"—imply
a return after death to the place of our racial origins.

But perhaps we are misled by our very instinct for arcadia,
and are therefore willing to accept an inauthentic substitute.
In our admiration of this prairie, are we not like children
gazing through the glass of a museum showcase? Is not the
restored prairie little better than a dusty little diorama, with
its perpetual brilliant sky lit dimly by the fluorescents, its
claustrophobic trompe l'oeil false perspective, its taxidermized
specimens frozen forever in some "natural" act of forage or
nestbuilding?

The preservationists of the old fire-and-brimstone school
would say just this. For them the discipline of ecology is essentially elegiac, essentially a eulogy to what we humans have
destroyed; their science is a postmortem, their myth is of a
primal crime by which we are all tainted, the murder of nature.
The best we can do to acknowledge our ecological sins—since
we cannot expiate, let alone compensate for them—is to set
aside whatever relatively untouched places remain and keep
human beings out of them. For such perfectionists the study of
nature is essentially passive and classificatory; action and
experiment would be unwarranted. A real diorama might not
disturb their fundamental sense of rightness so much as would
this restored prairie. A diorama, after all, does depict nature as
a corpse—a "nature morte," as the French call a still life. From
their point of view it would not falsify the truth so much as
does the apparently blooming health of the living imitation.

One can encounter the dismal grandeur of this position, its
Schadenfreude, in many sectors of art and learning. There are

performance theorists who regard the power relations of live performance as obscene; political purists who reject any reform as a palliative which will only delay the cleansing fires of the revolution; classicists who see only cultural decline since Homer; anthropologists for whom even their own presence in a traditional society is an irremediable taint to the purity of its unreflectivensss. Don't mess with Mother Nature. The opponents of genetic engineering are likewise haunted by the fates of Faust and Frankenstein. There are literary theorists who regard the process of verbal representation as a hegemonic power game designed to obscure the freeplay of reality, because language itself is an artifical ecology, and therefore essentially compromised. It is possible to sympathize with such a stance; those who hold it do indeed serve as a conscience to humankind.

But human beings are not at their best under the motivations of guilt and alarm. If not actually paralyzed, they act mulishly, dutifully, without the joy and playfulness that liberate the imagination and start the flow of creative thought. The result is specialization in knowledge and automatism in action.

Still, we cannot escape the awkward question: is the restored prairie a fake? One critic of restoration has argued that to have a restored coastline instead of a "natural" one is as if one's Vermeer were removed and secretly replaced by a perfect replica. One would be as shortchanged by the copy of nature as one would by the copy of the work of art. A large part of the value of a landscape, as with a Vermeer, is that it is the original; that is, its value depends on its origins.

This is a plausible and widely-held idea. Perhaps behind it we can glimpse the notion, fundamentally theological, that the world is a creation, and therefore inferior to its source, since the explanatory power of the creation would be quite void if there were properties in the creation which did not exist in the creator.

And under this notion there is, perhaps, that basic Indo-European habit of thought—perhaps a human habit of thought —that derives the nature of the child from the nature of the parent, and thus insists on the inferiority and subordination of child to parent. The very word "nature" is derived from an ancient Indo-European root meaning "birth," a root perhaps sounding like "gand," and giving rise also to such words as "natal," "native," "natural," and "nativity" on one branch,

"gender," "genus," "generate," "general," "genital," "gentle,"
"gene," and "generation" on a second branch, and the
Germanic "kin," "kind," "kindred" and "akin," on yet a third.
Even the practice of etymology as a pedantic explanation of
the meaning of a word implicitly privileges origins as determinative of outcomes.

But is not the true role of the parent to educate the child to
the point where it becomes independent of its origins, and
capable of creation beyond its parents' dreams? The American
Revolution was a declaration of such independence from the
motherland, the fatherland. And though there is one wisdom
that says that we know a thing by its grounds or origins, there
is another that says "by their fruits ye shall know them," that
derives the identity of something not from what produced it
but from what it produces. The kingdom of heaven may be
more like a mustardseed, like a leaven or ferment, than like an
achieved perfection; more in potential than in exhaustion of
possibility. The branching tree of evolution brings about wonderfully new forms of life, unpredictable from their origins
until they have actually appeared.

Perhaps we should think of a living landscape not so much
as like a Vermeer, but as like a sonnet, which, far from losing
when it is copied, derives its very life as a literary object from
its being printed and reprinted. Shakespeare has a sonnet (65)
that says just this:

> *Since brass, nor stone, nor earth, nor boundless sea,*
> *But sad mortality o'ersways their power,*
> *How with this rage shall beauty hold a plea,*
> *Whose action is no stronger than a flower?*
> *O, how shall summer's honey breath hold out*
> *Against the wrackful siege of batt'ring days,*
> *When rocks impregnable are not so stout,*
> *Nor gates of steel so strong, but Time dacays?*
> *O fearful meditation! Where, alack,*
> *Shall Time's best jewel from Time's chest lie hid?*
> *Or what strong hand can hold his swift foot back?*
> *Or who his spoil of beauty can forbid?*
> *O none, unless this miracle have might,*
> *That in black ink my love shall still shine bright.*

And it still does, unspotted by the centuries, precisely because
it has been copied and recopied in "black ink;" precisely

because it has taken on the ethic of the fruit and the seed, which is to give all to the future.

The analogy is a rather precise one. A landscape is not at all like a Vermeer if by that we mean that it is the same landscape year to year as a Vermeer is the same painting year to year. A prairie recopies, reprints itself every spring, using seeds and cuttings which are the books wherein are inscribed the instructions of the DNA code. A prairie is not so much like a Vermeer as like the renewing vision of the world that Vermeer began in our culture, that tradition of the revelatory power of light which is reborn in us every time we see a girl in a room lit by a tall window.

In reproducing a prairie, then, the ecological restorationists do but take a leaf out of nature's book. Nature copies; it is an *uncopied* prairie, if such could exist, that would be unnatural. When the retreat of ice caps, the silting up of lake beds, or devastation by volcanic ash lays bare a new environment suitable for prairie, the prairie species are seeded by natural vectors—wind, birds, insects—and copy themselves onto the empty page. Is not Homo sapiens in this case just another vector that the prairie biome employs to reproduce itself? A flower uses the esthetic preferences of the bee to attract its pollinator; likewise our esthetic attraction for the prairie causes us to carry its germs to a new environment.

But perhaps even this conception is too conservative. It is the job of the scholar to ensure that the sonnet remains utterly uncorrupted by copying or printer's errors; but nature's copying is not exact. Though the copying process is entirely natural— and thus the preservationist's argument against the "fake" is without substance—nature itself goes beyond copying to innovation, and allows copying "errors" into its sonnets in an attempt to improve them.

Let us be precise about this. A prairie grass can propagate itself in one of two ways: by cloning itself with runners or rhizomes; or by mating and sexual reproduction, using flowers, fruits, and seeds. When it sends out a new shoot, whether vertical, parallel to the ground, or under it, every biomolecular precaution is taken that the DNA in the new cells is identical to that in the originals. Redundancies in the code, periodic checks for exact matching in the complementary nucleic strands, and an immune system on guard against cancerous or virus-induced revisions of the code all protect the integrity of the copy. But when a plant reproduces itself sexually, the

policy is utterly changed. The twin strands of the chromo-
somes are unwound from each other, the naked strands are
paired with those of an alien individual, the genes are chopped
up and reshuffled, the copies are conflated and thus corrupted.
To an asexually reproducing organism such a procedure would
appear madness: if the purpose of reproduction is survival, this
deliberate self-infliction with cancer, this permission to an alien
virus to corrupt the code, would be suicide.

In one sense this is exactly the reaction of the strict preservationists to the work of ecological restoration. The preservationist philosopher I cited earlier compares the experience of
a restored landscape to that of a lover of nature who falls into
the clutches of a utilitarian-minded supertechnologist, who, by
means of an "experience machine" attached by electrodes to
the victim's head, is able to give him the illusory experience of
hiking through a spectacular wilderness. The horror implicit in
such a notion is like the horror of madness: we cannot correct
the error of our thinking because the correcting system itself is
damaged by the error. And sexual reproduction does just this
on the level of genetic information retrieval. The flavor of
paranoia in this analogy, the terror of losing one's identity,
might well be a survival into the realm of conscious feeling of
the xenophobic ethic of the immune system, which protects our
own self-cloning mechanism. An immune system without that
ethic is an immune system with AIDS.

Descartes, interestingly enough, used a similar thought
experiment (in his *Meditations on the First Philosophy* of 1641)
to prove that, though his senses might be totally deceived by a
demon, he could still think and therefore be. The only refuge
for the seeker after absolute truth lay in a conception of the
intellect that is essentially independent both of change and
appearance, and that operates in an eternal, immaterial world
of mathematics and logic. The senses are a trap. Sex, for the
biological organism as perhaps for the philosopher, seems to
threaten all consistency, all identity.

What, then, is sex for? Why should plants and animals go
to the extraordinary expense of complex energy-using reproductive systems, brilliantly pigmented or fluorescent scales and
plumage, flowers and fruit, courtship rituals and the rest, when
they could simply use their built-in growth system and bud
themselves a clone? It's all for one purpose: variation. To put
this more precisely, it is to create true genetic individuals. And
the function of individuals is to act as experimental tests of

various possibilities in body conformation, chemistry, and behavior that fall within the range of variation for the species. If the individual survives to reproduce, then its particular traits are perpetuated in the gene pool of the species. If it reproduces itself more abundantly than its parents, then it has probably found a better fit to the vicissitudes of its environment. In biological terms, the offspring can better represent its species than the parent. What this means is that, at least when dealing with the phenomenon of life and all phenomena derived from it (culture, technological development, religion, history, etc.), we must allow for the possibility that we can only truly understand something by knowing its future, its fruits, its consequences.

Even more revolutionary is the implication that the injunction to know things by their fruits and not only by their grounds might also apply to the inorganic world of physics and chemistry. The physical universe itself should then be characterized as being a life-producing universe. "Life-producingness," to follow this logic, is an essential trait of that species of one that we call the universe. This is a version of what physicists call the Anthropic Principle, which stipulates that one of the constraints on the initial state of the cosmos was that it should be the kind of cosmos that could bring about through evolution observers of it that could confirm its existence and compel it to actualize itself by observing it. Quantum theory treats reality as a coproduct of whatever is "out there"—in itself only a probability—and the act of observation or registering that forces the probability to collapse into actuality. Without observers—whether human or prehuman—no universe can exist.

This is a far cry from the ideas of the purists, who want us to leave Nature alone and who deplore the corruptions of human reflexiveness.

Our anxieties about this line of reasoning are not new. We do not like to bring our organs of knowledge into contact with our own origins; we are afraid that if we do we will poison our own source. The suspicion that we ourselves may be implicated in our own origins is blasphemous and frightening. The myth of Oedipus expresses that anxiety for the Greeks; and the myth of the nakedness of Noah expresses it for the Hebrews. Today we feel the same shudder at the idea of genetic engineering and the patenting of living organisms altered by recombinant DNA, and we think of Frankenstein. In each case a man

impiously comes to know the place whence he had his own
being, and is cursed for it; and in each case the implicit context
in one in which men have come to feel that they are in some
way authors of themselves.

But let us press on and see where the argument takes us.
Our meditation upon flowers is not yet over; for variation by
sexual recombination, which is the function of flowers, is not
enough by itself to keep the breed adaptively abreast of its
competition. Another element is required, and that is death. If
death does not cull out of the species those individuals whose
genes are not adapted to the environment, the defective genes
themselves will remain to contaminate the more vigorous
strains. It may seem paradoxical to describe death—which is
after all the opposite of survival—as a tool in the process of
evolution, whose mainspring is survival. But this is exactly the
magnificently risky policy to which the sexually-reproducing
organisms have committed themselves. Most sexual organisms
even contain a programmed aging system on the cellular or
genetic level to ensure that the individual does not outstay its
time. Sex and death are the two sides of the same system.

Aging, though, is not enough in many cases to clean out the
deadwood of genetic failure. Many prey species rely on their
predators to cull the unfit. As has happened many times in
managed wildlife preserves, the deer population of the Wisconsin Arboretum recently began to overflow the carrying
capacity of the land; in the long run such an unchecked population explosion would endanger the genetic vigor of the herd.
The effects of overpopulation unlimited by predation are similar
to the effects of incest and inbreeding in a human community:
individuals are born feebler, more susceptible to hereditary
diseases, and sometimes even deformed. The Arboretum prepared to shoot some of the deer to relieve the population
pressure. But now what some park managers call the "Bambi
Syndrome" set in. Public outcry against the deer kill was over-
whelming, and the Arboretum considered its options. (This
phenomenon is not confined to Wisconsin. Recently there was
so much fuss about the deer kill at a national zoological park
in Maryland that congressional hearings were held, with the
result that federal money was appropriated to evacuate the
deer and build a ten-foot steel fence completely round the park
to keep them from coming back. Democracy is sometimes a
beautiful thing.)

But not even predators are enough to keep the ecology

balanced. The old prairies were dependent on periodic fires to clear the thatch, fertilize the soil, and above all to kill the tree saplings that would otherwise quickly cover the ground. The richest mix of species only occurs on burnt prairies. Before the settlers came, a prairie fire could burn all the way from Illinois to the banks of the Wabash. In the words of William R. Jordan III, the editor of *Restoration & Management Notes,* "Remove the fires caused by lightning or set by Indians, and you have to replace them, or the prairie will quietly vanish, not in a roar of machinery but into the shadows of a forest." Accordingly the Wisconsin Arboretum burns its prairies every two years. It is said to be an unforgettable sight, with flames leaping up thirty feet, and it is gradually taking on the status of a ritual for the professionals and volunteers who supervise it. I myself can remember from my childhood in central Africa the spring burning practiced by the Ndembu tribe, and the air of festival it conveyed; it is associated for me with the smell of grass smoke, harsh native honey beer, the hunters' rites and dances, and the delicious little ground-fruits that we village boys would find among the burnt grass roots. Perhaps one day the prairie burning will be one of the great ritual and performative occasions of the midwest, a sort of festival of Dionysus the god of inexhaustible life, an occasion for drama, music, storytelling, poetry.

It is remarkable how passionate the true prairie restorationists, like William Jordan, Robert Betz at Fermilab, and Keith Wendt of Minnesota, are on the subject of burning. The discovery of the need to burn, I believe, was their great emancipation from the passivity of the naturalist, even a sacrificial rite of redemption for our ecological guilt. Even as the patient, careful labor of copying the natural prairie called for the medieval virtues—humility and obedience to nature, poverty and chastity of the imagination, the sensitivity and self-abnegation traditionally (and unfairly) assigned to the female gender, the self-effacement of the mystic and the scientist—the burning showed that nature needed us, needed even those most Promethean and destructive elements of our nature which are symbolized by fire.

All wise Arcadians know that Death is a welcome visitor there, and they resist any attempt to keep Him out. "Is there no change of death in Paradise?/Do ripe fruit never fall?" inquires Wallace Stevens; and our mythological heroes have gone so far as to eat the fruit, and die of it, to ensure Death's

place in Arcadia. And with death of course comes consciousness, reflection, that loss of innocence which makes Arcadia
capable of birth and creative novelty. The dream of the productive and creative Arcadia—as opposed to the sterile and
immortal place that always provokes us into rebellion and
fall—may now make more sense than we have given it credit
for. It is an ancient image of the garden that does not merely
freeze a moment of nature's being or capture the appearance of
nature, but does what nature does: reproduces itself, copies
itself into the future, and slowly improves on the copies by the
evolutionary play of mutation, sexual recombination, and selection. And now ecological restoration can give us the reality of
that image.

Some restorationists would argue that, though the sexual
and evolutionary elements of nature indeed exist, it is not the
job of restoration to promote them. The restored prairie should
be as much as possible a clone of the primordial prairie, and
the emphasis should be on ecology rather than evolution. But
others argue that the very reason we need the great restoration
projects with their thousands of hectares—the California red-
wood restorations, the restored wetlands, Dan Janzen's
visionary tropical dry forest restoration project in Costa Rica,
the "Bosques Colon" (Forests of Columbus) project in the West
Indies, the prairie restorations themselves—is to promote
genetic diversity and adaptability. The value is not merely to
act as museums but as active gene banks, with multiple alleles
and a strong repertoire of varieties and races ready to recolon-
ize the world when agriculture has progressed to the point
when it can share the land with them. Evolution is vital in the
short run as well as in the long: there are many species, like
the cheetah, which are threatened not by the diminution of
their numbers but by the lack of genetic diversity between
individuals. It is not enough, perhaps, entrusted with the
wealth of nature, to go and hide one's talent in the ground.

There may be ontological—even, in a way, religious—implications of this vision of things. In a very different field of
endeavor, the search for extraterrestrial intelligence, a shocking
conclusion is beginning to suggest itself, catalyzed by the awkward question blurted out a few years ago at an astronomical
conference: "Where is everybody?" Given the sensitivity of our
signal detection instruments, the ease by which radio signals
can be propagated to great distances, the huge number of
planetary systems within probable range of us, and the cer-

tainty that any other technological civilization must be employ-
ing radio frequencies for communication, the local airwaves
should be a gabble of interstellar chatter and TV transmission.
Instead, the silence is deafening. There is no sign that *anyone*
is out there. And the moment one begins to think about this
fact, it appears more and more plausible that we are alone in
the universe. For instance: it is now generally accepted that the
universe is only about twelve to twenty billion years old, but
estimates of how long it will remain in existence in such a
form as to support life range well over a hundred *trillion* years.
In other words, the universe has seen only a tiny fraction of its
existence; it is brand new. Why should we not be the first?
There has to be a first and, if we extrapolate our present rate
of technical advance, it need not be more than a couple of
million years before we will have populated the local galaxies.
Despite our long childhoods and small family size, like all
living organisms we multiply exponentially when there exists
no check on our living space. Two million years is a heartbeat
in cosmic time; the fact that no other intelligent species has
got here yet is almost proof that it doesn't exist. *We* would
have got *there*.

And consider this: given the present age of the universe,
there has only just been enough time, under the most favorable
conditions, for us to have evolved. First, the universe had to
cool enough to make possible ordinary stars. Then there had to
have been at least one previous generation of stars, which
lived out their life cycle, burned up their nuclear fuel, collapsed
and then exploded, to have produced the heavy element ash
out of which our own solar system is certainly made and without which no likely form of life could exist. Then the solar
system had to form. Almost immediately after the Earth cooled
down enough to support life, the first living organisms appeared, about four billion years ago, perhaps less than ten billion
years after the Big Bang. Earthly life has been around for
nearly a third of the universe's history. And yet all that time
was needed for life to transform the atmosphere from a
methane-nitrogen-water vapor-hydrogen sulfide-ammonia one
to a nitrogen-oxygen one, and to graduate from the very slow
evolution of asexual organisms to the rapid evolution of sexual
ones and the still more rapid evolution of social animals, whose
communities can to an extent evolve themselves. It would be
hard to imagine a faster evolutionary scenario than the one
that brought us into being on this planet.

If we are alone, then we carry a gigantic responsibility. We are the custodians of life in the universe, and the only plausible vector by which life may propagate itself to other worlds and thus escape the risk that some minor cosmic accident—the impact of a stray asteroid, or a disturbance of the sun's activity—should snuff out the first shoots of life forever. If this reasoning is correct, then the Earth will once more become what it was for the medieval imagination—the most important place in the universe. The theory of perspective tells us that the viewpoint of any observed scene is equidistant from all of its horizons; and thus, perhaps, since the universe borrows part of its existence from our observing of it, the medieval philosophers were partly right in putting the Earth at the cosmic center.

It is becoming clear that we cannot survive, psychologically or physically, without the rich web of other lives around us. If we leave this planet we must take our biosphere with us.

The great phylum of the angiosperms, the flowering plants, which appeared in the mid-cretaceous period and came in a mere five million years to dominate the ecology of the planet, owed its very existence to its insect assistants and the new ecological niches that they opened up. The simultaneous explosion of chordate species, of which we are one, may in turn be due to the richer carbohydrate and protein content of angiosperm seeds and fruits. The work of the bee and the bird in spreading angiosperm pollen and seed across the continents was not merely a conserving activity. Rather, it actively promoted the creation of new habitats and ecologically richer regimes. The ecological restorationists are taking the first step toward being able to reconstitute on some alien soil the elements of an earthly forest or prairie. Their distant successors will be like the bees, which serve as the gentle pander and reproductive vector of other species, but on a cosmic scale: participant-gardeners of nature.

The founders of Fermilab, the high-energy physics laboratory in Illinois, planted a tallgrass prairie—a gloriously lush and productive one—in the middle of the synchrotron accelerator ring itself. To be in that circular space, over a mile in diameter, is a peculiar experience. You can see on the horizon the low rampart housing the trillion-volt proton beam and its supercooled, superconducting magnets; but the place feels on a summer afternoon like a wild meadow with groves of giant oaks. One is reminded of those landscapes that they used to dream of before the death of the *Challenger,* those lakes and forests clothing the arched inner slopes of gigantic, slowly-spinning space habitats; where you could look up and see the other side of the world, like a real map, upside down over your head.

In Arizona a Texas millionaire is building an enormous cluster of glass vaults and domes, airtight and powered by the sun, which will house in miniature a mutually-supporting selection of all of the major biomes of the earth—rain forest, ocean, desert, steppe. It will be called Biosphere II; "Biosphere I" is what we are already living in. It will be inhabited by a team of young men and women who will eat what the environment produces, breathe the oxygen generated by its plants, drink what it has recycled, and fine-tune and garden the rest of their ecosystem. They will live in this terrarium for two years.

Perhaps our sense of wonder at these things is naive. Or perhaps it is one of those things whose loss is a bad bargain whatever you get in return. The issue is one of authenticity.

At present the restorationist bee is more necessary as a preserver than as a colonist; and the restorationist ethic is, as I have pointed out, one of a medieval self-effacement. This is as it should be. But the time may come when we, and our sister species of this planet, may seed ourselves across the solar system and beyond, as once the pelagic species colonized the land, and the insects and the birds and the air. The task will be enormous, and will be too much for the relatiely slow and unreflective processes of genetic adaptation. Who will write the *Georgics* of this new Arcadia? It will take wise bees, seed vectors of great exactness, able to provide the right environment for infant growth until the growth itself has altered those harsh environments into something hospitable to human beings. But one day the long discipline of restoration may bear a strange and unexpected fruit, and an alien sun may shine on miles of blowing prairie.

OPENINGS IN RELIGION

The third section, on religion, contains two essays, of which the first is a critique of modern religion both for its hostility to scientific revelation and for its neglect of its own traditional mysteries. This essay explores the thesis that the religious perspective is essential and deals with realities of supreme importance, even if they have not yet been accurately identified by theology.

A second essay, focusing upon the spirituality of Virginia Woolf and other rather unlikely and secular-minded thinkers, develops a conception of immortality and of the life of the spirit that fully meets the modernist criticism of religion while conserving and revivifying religion's ancient wisdom; certain feminist insights light the way.

6   The Future of the Gods

Notes toward a Postmodern Religion

Not long ago many educated people assumed that in the next few centuries religion would gradually disappear, to be replaced by a scientific philosophy, a secular and sociological ethic, and an existential esthetics. How dated this view now seems! Religion, far from being an epiphenomenon of socioeconomic and psychosexual forces, now clearly drives most of the world's political conflicts, economic choices, and styles of psychic being. Faced with the materially baseless prosperity of the Japanese and the suicidal sacrifices of the Shiites, we fall back on essentially religious language: "Confucian work ethic," "Islamic fundamentalism." Religion coexists very nicely, thank you, with modern science, technology, and war. It is obviously here to stay.

The anthropologists could have told us as much. We are a religious species; push the religious impulse down in one place, it pops up in another, sometimes the more dangerous and irrational because it is not recognized for what it is. Sex can be repressed or sublimated in a variety of fairly healthy ways, as the polymorphousness of human eros attests. But we repress the religious drive at our peril. Consider the massive changes in brain chemistry brought on by ritual trance, the astonishing feats of yogis and mystics, the addictive power of those narcotics and alkaloids that but feebly reproduce the "natural" rush of religious exaltation. Repress *those* instincts, bred into us by millions of years of prehistoric ritual practice with direct effects on reproductive success, and one finds oneself sitting on a time bomb.

The current prevalence of junk religions—the TV evangelists and fundamentalist sects, for instance—which proliferate like sugar-coated children's breakfast cereals, gives evidence of a deep human need for religion; if we can't get the real thing, we gobble down any trash that tastes like it. (Pregnant women, too poor and uneducated to feed themselves the proper vitamins their babies need, have been known to gorge on river clay and laundry starch.)

But the proponents of traditional institutional religion, who are or ought to be the custodians of imaginative psychic technologies of great age and effectiveness, should take little comfort in these observations. Why, after all, have the faithful not returned to them? The consumers of the junk religions, though they have obviously opted against secular modernism, have also opted against traditional institutional religion. It is time for traditional religion, and for all of us, to recognize that the whole current of major religions can change direction profoundly, and that such a change may now be long overdue. And by change I do not mean only the changes in theology and socioethics envisaged by feminist or liberation theology, nor the fundamental cosmological innovations proposed by evolutionary theology, process theology, and future theology, though they are straws in the wind.

What I mean is change on the order of the birth of Buddhism into the Hindu tradition, of Christianity into the Judaic, of Islam into medieval Arabia, or of Judaism itself into the polytheisms of the ancient Near East. Religion has changed radically in the past and will change again. To put it in religious terms, the spiritual history of the world is not over, and revelations as great as or greater than those given to us in the past may yet be in store.

One symptom of the coming changes is the vigorous religious syncretism now taking place in many parts of the world (and also the admiring recognition by anthropologists of the vitality of past syncretisms). Take for example the proliferation of Christian/animist/ancestor worship/witchcraft religions in sub-Saharan Africa, or Macumba in Brazil, or Baha'i in the West and Near East, or the various Christian/Buddhist/Traditional hybrids in Korea and Japan. I know a Jungian Catholic polytheist, an Iranian Sufi Hinduist Zoroastrian, an English Beshara Sufi Anglican pantheist, several Huichol Zen humanist nature worshippers, and a Catholic Baha'i transcendental mediator; my father's Catholicism was, he confessed, the closest thing he could find in the West to the richly ritual animism he had known as an anthropologist in Central Africa, and was tinged with ideas from Boehme, Blake, Marx, D. H. Lawrence, and Swedenborg. This new breed of syncretists are not kooks but people with a good sense of humor about their beliefs and a sound understanding of science.

How might we distinguish healthy syncretism from junk religion? The boundary is often vague, but one useful pointer is relative intellectual richness. Any religious practice that systematically diminishes the active human powers of thought and imagination is probably junk; it substitutes the death of the religious appetite for its satisfaction. Another pointer is the extent of internal dissent. A religion with too little authority generates no dissent but also few ideas; a religion with too much authority drives its dissenters out.

A third pointer is the extent to which a religion is fuelled by guilt and the need for security, that is, by fear of the past and the future. Guilt and alarm are very effective motivators, but they tend to kill out our sources of creativity and imagination. Guilt makes us mulishly expiate our sins, a beaten, duteous, unthinking animal; alarm makes us the victims of any masterful and self-confident protector. The new imperialism is the attempt, by manipulating their guilt and alarm, to suppress the inconvenient and enviable creativity of others. The guilty or alarmed person is docile, neutralized. Indeed, it was the fatal mistake of American political liberalism to rely for the implementation of its noble ideas on guilt and fear rather than imagination and hope; it turned liberalism into as much a junk religion as any sect of creationist fundamentalists. Genuine religion is playful, holy, reckless, and hilarious in all of its seriousness; the nature and meaning of the universe is risked, up for grabs, friendly only to the generous, the fools of god.

We are beginning to discover that—in the spirit of the Alfie character in the eponymous movie who maintained that the guts of a car are its upholstery—the guts of a religion are its rituals. By all means change the theology; this won't do any harm. Theology is the outward flourish and evanescent expressive form of a religion. Change the ethical system, if it has one, as long as our basic human-primate-mammal needs for food, families, and a creative arena are me.. we will change it anyway, and a religion that is slow on its feet is going to look hypocritical. Theology and ethics are discursive and subject to revision. That is why the great moral teachers spoke in parables; parables survive their original meanings. The kingdom of heaven is like unto a mustard seed, and will grow into something that looks quite different.

But where a religion really stands or falls is in its ritual. If it has good old rituals, carrying in them the inherited traces of our early evolution—the great psychic technologies of mythic storytelling, chant, sacrifice, body decoration, music, dance, the fresco—and if the best and most imaginative spirits have continuously been at work embodying the liturgy in new and inventive poetic performance, the theology and ethics will take care of themselves. Theology can then become what it ought to be, the most delightful and inspiring of all intellectual games; and the theory of ethics will be left to the real saints.

One might object to all of this that while it may be the case that psychological comfort, genetic inclination, and irresistible sociocultural tropisms are all served by religion, this does not make religion objectively true. Indeed, I might well be accused of maintaining a disingenuous stance: on the one hand celebrating the inevitability of religion in the human future, while on the other "explaining it away" by reference to brain chemistry and the evolution of the species, just as it was once explained away as fear of the unknown, technological incompetence, psychological dependency, or repressed libido.

But it is sign of the massiveness of the religious changes we are going through—changes in fundamental principles—that positions once regarded as inconsistent can now be perfectly logical. For instance, the term "objectively true" must, in an age of quantum mechanics and postrelativistic physics, either be discarded as the remnant of an old superstition or revised to accept a different content. What we can legitimately take as real depends on how it is measured, who is doing the measuring, in what spatiotemporal frame of reference, and with what set of assumptions, questions, and equipment. In a sense the whole universe is in an ongoing contest, or vote, or even free market, as to what ensemble of views of it will prevail as the canonical truth. Scientific experiment is only an acknowledgment that entities other than human beings—plants, animals, inanimate objects—have an "opinion" on what constitutes the universe, to be ignored at our peril. If truth is, as we now feel it to be, enacted into being by performative communities, we may define an object as a performative community.

Where such critics of science as Paul Feyerabend and Jean-Francois Lyotard go wrong is in thinking that human beings are the only such voters in the universe, and thus that science is reducible to a kind of sociology. (A friend reports to me on a recent meeting of a conference of humanists devoted to the philosophy of science: the proceedings were halted by the shocking suggestion that a person who jumped out of the window would fall down, instead of up or sideways, regardless of his or her sociopolitical orientation. The social construction of atoms and molecules would here, alas, overrule the social construction of persons).

"Truth," then, is the most effective view of the universe, measured in terms of whether its implications prevail in events (prediction); which is in turn measured by a consensus among the identifiable participants in the world, *human and non-human,* whose "opinions" on the matter can be canvassed.

If this definition is circular, it accords well with the feedback nature of physical processes as we now understand them in the work of such scientists as Ilya Prigogine and Mitchell Feigenbaum. Any *un*circular definition of truth must now be suspect. It is not now the *grounds* of an argument that prove its value, but its *fruits,* the richness of the field of topics that it embraces, the amount of sense it makes according to its own standards, the events that it unambiguously predicts.

Thus to describe religious experience in terms of brain chemistry, human evolution, and ritual behavior is not to diminish it but to extend the realm of its truth. The human brain is the most exquisitely sensitive instrument Nature has yet devised to make sense of and predict the behavior of the universe. It was produced by a ruthless selection process acting upon the richest and swiftest known collection of physical changes and recombinations, the biosphere of Earth. Any tendency in the human brain is *a priori* the result of a very powerful natural experiment in the production of accurate theories about the world: an inaccurate theorizing process is defined as a non-survivor in such an environment, while an accurate theorizing process will tautologously be strongly selected for.

If, then, the human brain has a chemistry and anatomy that makes it prone to developing religions, so that it does so independently again and again under different conditions, this is a very powerful argument that whatever religion is about is probably real. In like fashion we might say that the existence of ears argues for the reality of sound; and if we encountered a species with eyes, we would be most likely correct in assuming the presence of light in its environment.

This is not to say that what the religious "faculty" perceives is what religious people think it is. The variety of human religious beliefs and language is as remarkable as their universal presence; and, as in other areas of experience, we can legitimately argue with people's own identification of their experience. To say "the earth spins to face the sun" now agrees with a larger proportion of the world's vote than to say "the sun rises," which was once everybody's description of what they saw at dawn. And it predicts the future behavior of the world better. We can rightly contest religious dogmas without devaluing the reality that they attempt to verbalize. Religion is clearly about something real; the eyes and ears certainly see and hear something. What it is, we can continue to find out.

One implication of this argument is that it might be very rewarding to pay attention to the imagery of religion, even if we must sometimes reject religion's own interpretation of it. A patient who describes his pain as a burning knife under his lower ribs—or as the tooth of a dead hunter who is working witchcraft on him—may be giving very precise information to a doctor, in metaphorical terms. And metaphor may indeed in these cases be the *most accurate* form of language. Likewise we had better take very seriously the strange things that a religion says, though we could be very liberal in our interpretation of them. If they match what other religions say, and if they correspond with knowledge derived from other sources, like science, we should be especially attentive. The fact that believing in something, as William James pointed out, can help bring it about is not unconnected to the fact in quantum science that what we observe is partly determined by how we observe it.

But is not science itself in these terms a profoundly—even paradigmatically—religious activity? The historical accidents and failures of human imagination that resulted in the apparent opposition of religion and science may indeed have produced a linguistic anomaly, whereby the words themselves have become stunted, not being permitted to cover their natural range of expression; much human strife, self-deception, misery, and ignorance might have been avoided if the split had not occurred. But we do not need to accept this condition for ourselves. Perhaps the only difference between science and other religions is that the technology of science is not chiefly a technology of persons, a system for making the human brain more effective, but a technology of things. If Hinduism, for instance, uses advanced meditative and somatic techniques to achieve a psychospiritual control of the body, and Christianity uses the rites of communion to evoke the bonding energies of our familial/tribal past, science uses the protocols of experiment as a kind of ritual sacrifice whereby the hidden voice of nature is made to speak.

If religion is indeed preparing for a major paradigm shift, what should the new religious synthesis look like? One way to answer this question might be to list the requirements for a viable twenty-first century religion.

First, obviously, it should be syncretic. It should contain the best of the world's existing religions, without dilution to a watery deism carrying its own questionable metaphysical freight—monotheism, abstraction, the impersonality of the divine. The Irish and Roman priests who converted the Anglo-Saxons to Christianity, the Jesuits who converted the Indians to Catholicism, the Buddhist evangelists in China and Japan, all managed rich and satisfying blends of their faiths with the indigenous cults. If the project of synthesis appears difficult, it is; but the polytheisms of ancient Greece, ancient Rome, and India all achieved it more or less, and stand as great reproaches to the monstrous human scandal of religious war. What do we have brains for but to reconcile the irreconcilable? A successful syncretism would have the added virtue of dispelling that vulgar and convenient excuse of doubt based on the cultural varieties of religion, which is really a permission to the self to avoid the high and demanding work of soul-construction.

The new religion should, moreover, exploit to the full the ancient psychic technologies deployed in traditional ritual practice. Those elements of the contemporary arts which are genuine extensions and developments of the fundamental human grammars of creativity should rejoin their parent stem of ritual and spiritual practice. The irreverence, charivari, grotesqueness, and comedy that Mikhail Bakhtin celebrates as characteristic of healthy ritual traditions should be revived, so that the moments of holiness and ecstasy should have a sure foundation in the sensuality and critical intellect of our species. At the same time that the ancient texts and liturgies are revived, a new playfulness should enter our ritual observance. The energy of performance, which animated the chorales of Bach as it does the painted dance of the cargo cult, should be renewed.

It is high time that the institutions of religion, instead of lagging complainingly behind the new religious revelations as they come pouring out of science, take their proper place at the leading edge of science, as they used to do. To catch up, theology must transform itself so as to be in accord with the spirit of contemporary science.

Cosmological physics tells us that the universe began in chaos and inarticulacy, and shaped itself into its present consummate order and beauty by mechanisms and drives that are not supererogatory but logically inherent in the process itself. (Let me refer here to two excellent books: Ilya Prigogine's *Order Out of Chaos* and Paul Davies's *God and the New Physics*.) Any creator we seek to know through her or his creation takes on as properties the fundamental principles of the created thing. The deterministic and tyrannical God of the eighteenth century is a reflex of the deterministic physics that was erroneously thought to govern the world. Likewise if we insist that God must be the creator of the universe, the only creator the new universe would need, if it needed one at all, would be a chaotic and incoherent one; the physical constants, the enabling conditions for the subsequent history of the universe, could all, in the view of many scientists, have arisen by a process of selection for endurance and mutual agreement that would operate on its own. If we persist in seeking God in the pastward direction of time, before rather than after, we will find only a moron god, a god for elementary particles and not for plants, animals, and human beings.

Perhaps what we want is a polytheism in which we include that god in our pantheon. But then we should also find a place for a god of growth, of self-articulation, of cumulative reflexivity and utterance, the spirit of the evolutionary heart of nature, and nature's software, the human species. Jesus likened the kingdom of heaven to a yeast, a mustard seed, to the intricate processes of growth; and in the parable of the sower, we find a graphic image of the process of evolution by natural selection. Such a god would be located not in the past of the world but in its ever-incipient present: a pillar of cloud by day, going on before the people, and a pillar of fire by night. And in this pantheon we might even find a place for that god who is named by denial—the Tao that is not the Tao if it can be spoken, the sound of one hand clapping, Job's god whose ways are not to be understood by created beings. That god would be the darkness of the future, the vacuum that draws out being into itself, the incompleteness of things that makes possible new events.

But if in our defense of the Divine we relieved it of the

degrading burden of being the originator of the universe, there is still something valuable, something profound, in the idea of a creator. Might we not take the word "creator" as "caller into being," the maker of sense out of things, as the eye calls into being the colors, and as the word makes sense of the world? Might we not thus recover the seed, the ovum, of meaning in the idea of God as the word, as the logos? Then our miraculous possession of all of those languages—poetry, mathematics, painting—would place us as the very temples of the creator; as the Brihad-Aranyaka Upanishad and the New Testament remind us, the kingdom of heaven is within us. Could this be another description of that growing, historical god of the incipient present? After all, the Latin root for meaning—"sem" —also means seed; and the "matter" of an utterance, as opposed to its outer form, is cognate with the matrix, the womb.

Likewise, when we consider quantum physics, we see the universe as a field of possibility which is embodied and given effect by the act of observing, so that the present moment takes form as a wave of actuality, what Whitehead called concrescence. Here again we might articulate our theology in such a way as to bring out the wisdom of ancient dogma—the divine as unknowable essence and as incarnate word, spirit, and avatar: the infinite possibility of an untampered-with electron, and the actualizing fiat by which it comes into being as a definite event in space and time.

Perhaps most exciting of all, we have in the fact of evolution a characterization of the divine spirit which is fully satisfying to the religious faculty. The capacity of the evolutionary process to generate more advanced, beautiful, and self-reflexive lifeforms out of more primitive, incoherent, and automatic ones corresponds nicely to the theological insistence on the goodness and generosity of God. The open-endedness of evolution, its ability to produce radically novel entities, corresponds to the notion of the creator. Likewise, this radical novelty also implies freedom, for what is freedom if it is not the power to create new entities? Mere choice between existing alternatives is either random—an "acte gratuite" as the existentialists say— or deterministically constrained by preference or inclination. Neither of these constitutes freedom; it is amazing that Camus and Sarte, who were intelligent men, could image that the way out of the determinist trap should be by random choice. It is as if one were to escape death by claiming to be a stone, which cannot die. In evolution religion has finally found a defense of one of its most dearly-held principles, freedom. This is why I would take "scientific creationism" to be a sign of junk religion: it denies the characteristic hallmark—the personal signature—that the divine makes in the world, the beautiful mark of freedom.

If we extend the idea of evolution to cover also the adaptive/ variative process by which we cultural beings generate new conceptions, we may say that new thoughts, personalities, and works of art are essentially new species, generated so much more swiftly than genetics permits. And here again the religious language of the vedas and the gospels, of the spirit as within, as a seed, is beautifully borne out, and in a way which is concrete, immediate, more actual than any metaphor. Eternity is that intenser form of time which is as much advanced beyond ordinary human time as human time is advanced, in the evolutionary order, beyond the time of animals.

Perhaps these remarks occasion a kind of disquiet, a queasy feeling about the disturbance of roots, the shifting of ground. But perhaps that feeling is essential to religion, and is one of the components of the sacred. Should we have as much control over our religion? But is it not in the fear of our own freedom that we encounter the terror and joy of the divine?

7   The Immortal Conversation

Culture as the Web of Talk

In Virginia Woolf's *The Waves* we hear the voice of a sort of super-soul, made out of seven individual persons, seven friends. Each contains a complete if blurred image of the others, and the coherent light of Woolf's prose reconstitutes out of them the original shapes of their personal identity.

The poet John Donne also meditated upon the spiritual union of persons; when love, as he says in "The Ecstasy," "inter-inanimates two souls, /That abler soul which thence doth flow/ Defects of loneliness controls." Donne had much traffic with nothingness, and it seemed to him that the loneliness of the individual soul is its chief defect; and thus a perfect soul could not be lonely. Finding company only among its own kind, and divided from other souls by its embodiment in flesh, the only perfect soul is a composite soul, a unity transcending the separateness of persons, as the unity of a person transcends the variety and perishability of the bodily organs of which that person is made. Unlike the ordinary individual soul, which cannot experience the mechanism by which its components, the physical organs, operate, that new composite soul would be able to know by introspection the operations of its own ele-ments, because its elements would be souls like itself. Because the soul of each friend or lover participates in a super-soul which contains both, its essential identity survives the death of the body of which it is made.

Virginia Woolf puts this conception to the severest test in *The Waves* by having one of those friends, Percival, die, and then measuring rather precisely the extent to which his identity is lost from the conversation altogether, or preserved in the shared self-substance of the survivors. She does something of the same in *To The Lighthouse;* when Lily Briscoe finally finishes her painting, it is with a stroke which describes both the absence and the continued presence of the dead and much-beloved Mrs. Ramsay. Can we imagine that whatever sanity there might have been in Woolf's suicide was some kind of existential test of the same set of ideas? And is she not in some way vindicated in her belief, as she stands before us, almost too beautiful and eccentric for us to see her clearly, but unmistakably there, when we listen to her style:

> Oh Mrs. Ramsay! she called out silently, to that essence which sat by the boat, that abstract one made of her, that woman in grey, as if to abuse her for having gone, and then having gone, come back again. It had seemed so safe, thinking of her. Ghost, air, nothingness, a thing you could play with easily and safely at any hour of the day or night, she had been that, and then suddenly she put her hand out and wrung the heart thus. Suddenly, the empty drawing-room steps, the frill of the chair inside, the puppy tumbling on the terrace, the whole wave and whisper of the garden became like curves and arabesques flourishing round a centre of complete emptiness. *(To the Lighthouse,* 1927; New York: Harcourt Brace, 1955, p. 266.)

And there she is, Mrs. Woolf for us, as Mrs. Ramsay for Lily Briscoe.

But to come back from the dead is no easy matter. *Hoc opus, hic labor est,* says Virgil; this is the work, this is the task. Virgil himself, perhaps, managed that remarkable trick when Dante met him in the dark wood of his mid-life; and Dante in turn, with a Florentine freedom of gesture that he lent to Virgil in his poem, has taken the hand of later poets as various as William Blake and T. S. Eliot. But what is the work, the labor?

Now here we must do some very careful thinking, so that we may very well feel in a dark wood ourselves, far away from the light and obviousnes to us of Lily Briscoe's and Virginia Woolf's achieved vision. That vision is bought and paid for; let us find out the price.

Those friends, first of all. Percival, Mrs. Ramsay, Mrs. Dalloway, have been able to make and keep a circle of friends, and this has something to do with their ability to come back from the dead. Virginia Woolf herself was a member of a very remarkable group of friends: Duncan Grant, Vanessa Bell,

Bertrand Russell, Roger Fry, G. E. Moore, John Maynard Keynes, Vita Sackville-West, Lytton Strachey and others; a group that was also connected with T. S. Eliot, Ludwig Wittgenstein, Sigmund Freud, and the leading social reformers, scientists, and critics of the time.

Is fame, then, the way one comes back from the dead? I think not. These are indeed famous people, but the feeling we got listening to Virginia Woolf's prose had nothing to do with fame. Nor is intellectual brilliance enough for that return journey. Mrs. Ramsay is not especially intelligent or knowledgeable. In the matter of death, although we must think hard, we must be guided by our feelings.

Let us go directly to the point. Does the soul survive the body? What is the soul? What does its survival—if it survives, and if it exists—have to do with those friends? Now the spirit of Bloomsbury was a spirit of radical skepticism in religious and spiritual matters. Russell sought to reduce all thinking to facts logically connected. Keynes is the supremely secular economist. The others were all atheists or agnostics of one kind or another, and saw it as a point of honor to face death squarely, a death which meant the end of personal continuity and subjective consciousness. In the spirit of Bloomsbury, let us see what of the soul and spirit are attainable or even desirable within the limits of the human understanding of the world. In this game it is cheating to invoke the possibility of purposes or essences beyond the human understanding. (In other games it is cheating if we don't; but they are other games.) Wittgenstein said it very simply: the limits of my language are the limits of my world; and whereof one cannot speak, thereof one must remain silent. Let us set aside for the moment the extremely important fact that in speaking of that of which one cannot speak he is breaking his own rule, and in describing the limits of the world he must perforce be stepping outside of them far enough to recognize them as limits. Let us play the game.

What, then, would a modern hard-science brain anatomist say about the soul? Roger Sperry, the Nobel-prizewinning brain scientists, sees the nervous system as a hierarchy of causations, the earliest and most primitive of which are subsumed into and governed by those which are evolutionarily later and more advanced. I have taken the following quotations from the remarkable book *Nobel Prize Conversations*.

Above simple pain and other elemental sensations in brain dynamics, we find, of course, the more complex but equally potent forces of perception, emotion, reason, belief, insight, judgment and cognition. In the onward flow of conscious brain states, one state calling up the next, these are the kind of dynamic entities that call the plays.

It is exactly these encompassing mental forces that direct and govern the inner flow patterns of impulse traffic, including their physiological, electro-chemical, atomic, subatomic, and subnuclear details. It is important to remember in this connection that all the simpler, more primitive, elemental forces remain present and operative; none has been canceled. These lower-level forces and properties, however, have been superseded in successive steps, encompassed or enveloped as it were, by those forces of increasingly complex organizational entities. For the transmission of nerve impulses, all of the usual electrical, chemical, and physiological laws apply, of course, at the level of cell, fiber and synaptic junction...

Near the apex of this compound command system in the brain we find ideas. In the brain model proposed here, the causal potency of an idea, or an ideal, becomes just as real as that of a molecule, a cell, or a nerve impulse. Ideas cause ideas and help evolve new ideas. They interact with each other and with other mental forces in the same brain, in neighboring brains, and in distant, foreign brains. And they also interact with real consequences upon the external surroundings to produce in toto an explosive advance in evolution on this globe far beyond anything known before, including the emergence of the living cell. (Sir John Eccles, Roger Sperry, Ilya Prigogine, Brian Josephson: *Nobel Prize Conversations,* Dallas: Saybrook, 1985, 59 ff.)

This is not an extreme view among brain scientists. There are still indeed some traditional materialists who, despite the recent dethronement of matter as the fundamental causal force of the universe, would deny the causal power of the higher integrations of brain function. But on the other hand there are also scientists, like Sir John Eccles, who would find Sperry's insistence on the immanence of mind in brain too cautious, and would argue frankly for a nonmaterial mind. In a sense the argument is the same as the one conducted in the house of Socrates the night before he was to drink the hemlock of his punishment by the Athenian State, recorded in the *Phaedo*. Is the soul a mixture, an attunement, or an independent entity? Is it immortal?

The answer of the brain scientists seems to be that the mind—"soul" is a word they avoid, but they use "mind" to mean much the same thing—is an attunement, a harmony, in Socrates' terms. That is, the mind is like the state of attunement of a musical instrument, which is not the pegs, sounding board, and strings, nor the wood that they are made of, but a particular arrangement of their mutual tensions and relations. For Sperry and others that arrangement may itself be capable of action and govern the behavior of the components of the instrument; but "the conscious self does not survive brain death." Nevertheless, Sperry by implication leaves open, in the passage I have cited, the possibility that, to the extent that the brain of one person is able to imprint itself on the brains of others, that imprint might survive; and he goes on to speculate that it is precisely the highest integrations of mental life that can survive in this way:

> One looks...to the higher special peaks in the mental life, and not to the living neural substrate of these but to the transcendent mental content itself that emerges at the very top of the multinested neuro-molecular-atomic-subatomic brain hierarchy. On such terms one can infer that perhaps the essence of the very best of the conscious self of Beethoven, of Shakespeare, Michelangelo, etc., are still with us.

But here Sperry runs into the same difficulty we encountered before; surely we are not here talking about fame? Sperry admits it, but concludes:

> We can't all be Beethovens, of course, or Leonardos, or Edisons, or Darwins, etc., but there are ways in which the highest aspect or form of the conscious experiences of each individual can realistically be extended in this manner to exist beyond death of the neural substrate that originally sustained it. (Ibid, p. 168 ff.)

What ways, though? One day, perhaps, as science fiction writers have speculated, we will be able to download the characteristic pattern of nerve impulses that constitutes a person into an electronic recording, which might be replayed on an enormously powerful computer. One problem with this idea, once we have overcome a sort of superstitious repugnance to it, is the sheer amount of information that would need to be recorded. The brain is capable of ten to the ten to the ninth power states of consciousness—that is, ten followed by a billion zeros, more zeros than you could print in a thousand books.

But on the other hand, the mathematical laws governing the Fourier transform allow for the expression of any finite ensemble of information, of any complexity, to be expressed in terms of a curve. Human beings have a marvelous capacity to generate unique curves: the unmistakable shapes of a person's handwriting, or of the painter's or the potter's hand. In a sense all of our heredity and all of our experience go into such a curve. Perhaps it is not too fanciful to imagine that within the shard of pottery shaped by a neolithic potter there is enough information to completely reconstitute her, flesh, bone, personality, and all, if we only knew how to extract and embody it.

Ancient vibrations recorded by chance on sensitive media are now being restored by scientists. I have heard a piece of Roman pottery being used as a gramophone record, the grooves around its edge being "played" by a laser "needle," and could hear the regular thud of the treadle being worked two thousand years ago, and a vague sound, which the acoustic scientists distinguished from the noise made by the process itself, that might have been the ambient vibrations of the workshop—perhaps including a fragment of speech or song. Will we one day be able, in some kind of marvelous sonic archeology, to reconstitute from the acoustic traces of the past the very objects that made the sounds?

A more serious objection to the idea that human personality can be reconstituted from an inanimate physical recording of it is that the process of reconstitution would require a machine, a calculator, more powerful than anything in the physical universe. The number of electrons in the universe is much smaller than the number of thoughts a human brain is capable of. Thus it would indeed take a divine, transcendent, and super-universal being—but not necessarily an infinite one!—to play back the traces we have left so as to put Humpty Dumpty together again. But at least in theory the world does contain sufficient recording space to preserve through their mortality a certain essence of entities as complex as a human personality.

Consider for instance the mortality of our own bodies while we are alive. I mean the death of the cells which goes on throughout our lives, and which completely recycles all of the matter in the body every seven years. Given a calculator as powerful as a human being's genetic and nervous machinery, and designed precisely for the purpose, the recording of the past state of a human mind and body can be reconstituted satisfactorily. Though the body I was born with is now dead, and so, alas, are five of its successors, somehow the entity which is Frederick Turner got printed onto new material so accurately that I keep even my scars, and recognize my remembered seven-year old self as unmistakably me.

But eventually the baton of awareness can no longer be passed on to new living tissue, and it must surely fall. If the only calculator capable of reconstituting the recorded information that specifies a human personality is the brain and body of the very human personality in question, then physical immortality is impossible. Nevertheless there is evidence pointing to the likelihood that something can be passed on, even if it is not subjective consciousness. Why not subjective consciousness? some will ask. Let them reflect how fragile consciousness is. Not even a perfectly healthy and alive human body is sufficient to maintain the flame of awareness; when we are in a dreamless sleep, our conscious selves do not exist. We even recognize this fact legally when we permit some patients in a terminal coma to pass away before the last moment to which their organic existence can be prolonged. If it takes only the shutting down of certain minor brain centers to render the conscious self utterly void, what must be the effect of the complete cessation of brain activity?

Still, the greatest masters and mistresses of the wisdom of death tell us with unmistakable authority that something is not lost in death.

I myself have a personal interest in this question. Some years ago my father, the anthropologist Victor W. Turner, died in his home in Charlottesville. He was a rare human being; it would be a very great pity if his peculiar outlook on things, his appetite for all things human, his wit, his unconscious goodness, his self-distrust, his marvelous sense of ridiculous comedy, were lost forever to the world. I have caught myself sometimes speaking with his voice, being cautioned to think twice about a

cheap position in an argument, finding something wonderfully
funny in a way which is V. W., not F., Turner. I have even had
long conversations with the old man on the word procesor.
Perhaps the dead are printed in the brains of the living.

Consider: a patient afflicted with split personality can maintain several distinct persons, quite autonomous of one another,
with the same brain tissue. It looks as if the difference between
us and such patients is that we keep our subjective center
inside just one of the huge symbol-systems that constitute persons within our brains—the one labeled "I;" while the pathological mind cannot control that center, and it runs away and
inhabits the different selves that we carry within us. But this
implies that we do contain all the raw material and equipment
for the full operation of selves different than ourselves. Some
of those selves are potential versions of ourselves; but others
are indeed miniature programs for other people altogether. It
seems likely to me that one of Virginia Woolf's pathological
symptoms was a tendency of that center to wander; a problem,
perhaps, peculiarly dangerous for a novelist, who must live her
characters' lives almost as intensely as her own. Actors, too,
are prone to this tendency; as Hamlet says,

> *Is not monstrous that this player here,*
> *But in a fiction, in a dream of passion,*
> *Could force his soul so to his own conceit*
> *That from her working all the visage wann'd,*
> *Tears in his eyes, distracion in his aspect,*
> *A broken voice, an' his whole function suiting*
> *With forms to his conceit? (Hamlet, II.ii. 556)*

Henry David Thoreau muses on the strange doubleness in
ourselves, that sometimes makes us strangers to ourselves.
Indeed, if we did not possess it we might not be capable of
meditation or even of conscious reflection. Our lives, he says,
are like a play, which we observe sometimes with the deepest
involvement, sometimes with a rather chiling and inexplicable
detachment.

The brilliant mathematical psychologist Vladimir Lefebvre
explains our capacity to make balanced moral judgments by
reference to semiautonomous representations of other people
that we maintain in our brains. How else indeed do we see ourselves as others see us? Freud more gloomily described the
process of internalization and introjection by which the desires

and intentions of another person—especially one of our parents —might come to act the tyrant within a person's unconscious. But might there not be a gloriously healthy and indeed almost heavenly version of this same process? Do we not feel that we possess a little piece of our beloved, and he or she possesses a little piece of us? And is there not something beautifully symbolic of love in the fact that a man can leave something of himself with a woman, which will, united with something of her own germ-stuff, become a person in its own right?—that can be born even after its father has died? Religion is seldom entirely foolish in its ritual activities; consider ancestor-worship in China and other Oriental cultures. Does not this practice reflect an intuitive truth about the way we feel for the beloved or revered dead?

Perhaps the answer lies in the nature of the community within which a person's being is recorded. Religion speaks of a "communion of saints," a "mystical body." Dante evokes this richly in the *Purgatorio* and *Paradiso,* and distinguishes its animating principle—that is, love—sharply from fame; though even in hell fame has its proper prerogatives. If during a person's life his or her own body is sufficient to preserve and reconstitute, even after several hours of sleep, the continuity of personal consciousness, perhaps other persons can to some extent perform the same office for a human being who is going through that last sleep of all; perhaps after death we do wake again in some sense, in the consciousness of other people. This idea resembles the Hindu and Buddhist notion of reincarnation, but it requires a conversation between the dead (when they were alive) and the living. Let us examine the conversation that constitutes this immortality, and those circles of friends that have carried on the conversation.

I have been collecting such groups, and very interesting they are. Virginia Woolf, who comes as close as anyone in encountering without wishful thinking the lived experience, so to speak, of immortality, was, as we have seen, a member of a wildly various group of artists and intellectuals. Such a group existed also in Shakespeare's time, and it included the likes of Walter Raleigh, John Florio the translator of Montaigne, the playwright Christopher Marlowe, the great scientist and mathematician Thomas Hariot, the astronomer Giordano Bruno, the Wizard Earl of Northumberland, George Chapman the translator of Homer, the artist Nicholas Hilliard, the navigator Humphrey Gilbert, the young John Donne, and many others: poets, scientists, political theorists, explorers, philoso-phers. We find a similar constitution among the membership of Goethe's circle, among the Florentine Neoplatonists, in the group that Castiglione pictures for us in the lovely Umbrian castle that is the setting for *The Courtier,* in the circle of Cicero, in the great academy of Alexandria that Queen Berenice brought together, and of course in the academy of Athens. Here in America we may cite the Transcendentalists, the circle of Emerson and Thoreau, as a comparable example.

These groups all share recurring themes. First, as is obvious, they are all radically interdisciplinary. Can this feature have anything to do with the theme of immortality? Let us leave this intriguing question for a moment and look at certain other characteristics possessed in common by such circles of friends.

They all share an interest in death; not a morbid interest only, but an adventurous curiosity, an anticipation, a fear modified by the good company they feel they will have in that last journey. They talk about dead sages and artists, and try to resurrect their spirit in thier own times, and they consider their own deaths with a frankness and courage which stirs our imaginations: for example Socrates' grand myth of death in the *Phaedo,* Raleigh's poem written on the day before he went to the scaffold, the soliloquy of Marlowe's Faustus as he awaits the last coming of Mephistophilis.

A strong case could be made that these groups have acted as profoundly creative sources of ideas for their whole culture, have set the agenda for future dialectic, and stood as criteria of artistic and intellectual achievement for future generations. Yet in most cases we know of their existence obliquely; they did not publish their proceedings, and we must rely on the good luck of there being present a Plato, a Castiglione, a Boswell to write it down; or glean the gist of the talk from letters, journal accounts like Bruno's *Cena della Ceneri,* or even the philosophical soliloquies of Shakespeare, which, I believe, drew on Shakespeare's own personal experience of the School of Night, as the circle was called. In any case, the conversation was essentially an oral one, not a written one. So our search for immortality has led us to the most evanescent and transient of activities: talk.

How can talk be the medium of anything as durable as immortality? To answer this question we need to strike out in a new direction. Almost all of the serious thinkers who have examined cultural and intellectual history have found themselves forced into postulating the existence of some huge and overriding force, largely autonomous at its own level of operation, which seems to coordinate the ideas of a given historical period. Hegel calls it the *Zeitgeist,* the spirit of the time. Burkhardt's description of the Renaissance is in terms of a succesion of dominant mental styles; and his ideas perhaps derive from those of Vico, who saw civilization proceeding in cycles of barbarism, heroism, and reason. Alfred North Whitehead writes of "views of the world," "climates of opinion," and Thomas Kuhn describes science as being dominated by "paradigms" of verification and experiment. Carl Jung identifies a collective unconscious, though he did not see it as evolving with cultural evolution. Yeats, following the Rosicrucian tradition, calls it the Spiritus Mundi.

Now why should these thinkers, so various and independent in their speculations, have fallen upon a similar hypothesis to explain their findings? It must be that when history is considered globally, the individual events no longer appear merely coincidental; it is like one of those blown-up photographs which, when you look at it up close, seems nothing more than a random collection of dots and splotches, but when you step back it resolves itself into a picture—a picture sometimes remarkably sharp and full of detail. There really is a Zeitgeist, then, and it is not the mere additive sum of its details. It has an independent power of its own and can influence events. Does this mean, though, that we must now violate the rule we made for ourselves, that we should not assume the existence of anything beyond human understanding? Must we stand at the edge of thought, wring our hands, and consign ourselves to mysticism? Must we accept our actions and thoughts as governed by an ineffable supervening force which does not yield to explanation?

Perhaps not; or not yet, at any rate. There is an interesting resemblance between the idea of the Spiritus Mundi, the Zeitgeist, and a concept we have already touched on, that is, the way that the brain's individual neurons, each obeying the laws of cellular metabolism, can in aggregate carry and maintain a consciousness, intentions, and ideas that in turn are determinative of the states of the neurons themselves. What I am suggesting is that there is a Zeitgeist, and that it is not ineffable at all. The Zeitgeist is constituted by that very web of conversation that I referred to before. Each age of culture and thought has at its core a conversation, centered perhaps on a few individuals, mediated by the sensitive atmosphere of friendship, and extending outwards to include the whole language-community. Talk is to historical events as mind is to brain.

The channels by which these superindividual but quite unmysterious entities communicate themselves throughout a culture are well known. Everybody in America, for instance, knows everybody else at five removes. That is, given any person on the continent, I know someone who knows someone who knows someone who knows that person. In most cases the connection is even closer. Even a person of rather limited political contacts probably knows at least one person who has had the ear of President Bush. Consider the superconductive volatility of jokes and rumors and catchphrases and idioms, even when they don't make it onto television until they are passé. Among children it's staggering, and international; I have heard new jokes being told, a few days apart, in England and America. Everybody knows everybody in the world at ten removes.

Most talk merely transmits existing ideas and thoughts rather than originating them. But even the most casual talk is original in little ways; the requirements for improvisation are so enormous, and the human context so unique and various, that no word can ever be used in exactly the same sense as it has before, and thus every use of a word is somewhat metaphorical. Moreover the human palate and ear are so variable that little phonological changes can continually accumulate, until they are large enough to drive semantic changes—as when a word alters to the point where it sounds like another word and begins to be colored by its meaning. But this level of originality is very much slower and more impersonal than the kind that burns so brightly in the great core conversations of a culture, and that acts as the spark plug for the Zeitgeist as such.

Can it be that talk of this kind has a life of its own which transcends the individuals by which it is generated? That though its particular instantiations are momentary and fleeting, it is carried in people's brains in the form of ideas? "Ideas" seems not quite the right word; an idea is something complete and thus not entirely compelling. Are they not rather, perhaps, profound and nagging questions which will not let us go and which are a pleasure to return to, because they are always being solved but are never finished with, and are always illuminating other problems? And when there is an encounter with another member of the great conversation, out comes that question again, with sweet climbing masses of the blossom of other personalities attached—even the personalities of the dead.

Beautiful though this conception is, we may discover a number of objections to it. Could we not protest that this kind of immortality is immortality for great minds? Not fame, indeed, but still something that it takes talent for, and perhaps genius, and education, and the confidence of a spirit that has never felt itself mastered by another? And, as Virginia Woolf points out in *A Room of One's Own,* the leisure and cultivation and access to great minds of the past that this kind of immortality seems to require have been until recently the prerogative largely of the male sex.

An even more disturbing objection might be that if the participants in this conversation, this inner life of the Zeitgeist, are truly like mere neurons in a brain, does not the immortality of the conversation utterly negate that individuality, and, most important of all, that freedom for which we value human beings? Are we not then mere automata, in the grip of gigantic and incomprehensible historical forces? Yeats's symbol for this overcoming by history is a rape—the rape of Leda by Zeus in the form of a swan. "Being so caught up,/ So mastered by the brute blood of the air," he asks, "Did she put on his knowledge with his power/ Before the indifferent beak could let her drop?"

And what if those historical forces are knowable, as Karl Marx believed?—the forces of class struggle, economic determinism, the drive of dialectical materialism toward the dictatorship of the proletariat? Does not that superindividual force turn us into conscienceless killers, remorseless instruments of a faceless economic justice, tools of the party line? It is no coincidence that Marxist psychology labels individuality a sort of bourgeois disease, a false consciousness that must be rooted out at its source. The worst excesses of the true believers in the divine plan, the Islamic, Christian, or Jewish fundamentalists, are not so cruel as those of the serious and committed historicist.

Let us grant that Marxism is a hideous caricature of that conversation. I hope the idea still attracts us with its promise of insight yet undiscovered, insight that will resolve our objections, even the problem of its moral unaccountability. Still, another objection looms: even if the conversation survives the death of a participant, it cannot preserve the identity of the dead from the subsequent decay of time. As Woolf puts it in *To the Lighthouse:*

> But the dead, thought Lily, encountering some obstacle in her design which made her pause and ponder, stepping back a foot or so, Oh the dead! she murmured, one pitied them, one brushed them aside, one had even a little contempt for them. They are at our mercy. Mrs. Ramsay has faded and gone, she thought. We can override her wishes, improve away her limited, old-fashioned ideas. She recedes further and further from us... (Op. cit., p. 260.)

Our quest, then, our search or pursuit seems to have come up empty. We might well feel disheartened by the turn we have taken. But let us remember old Socrates, who caught his beloved disciples at just such a juncture in their quest for the nature of the soul in the *Phaedo;* how he rallies his friends and bids them not to give up yet though the day is almost over and the State will come soon to claim the debt to which Socrates has signed his soul. Let us be rallied at they were, and go on with the enterprise to the last.

There was a loose end that we left earlier, a curious characteristic of those circles of friends we examined, that we passed over, partly perhaps because it seemed too dry and intellectual to give us what we sought. Those groups were interdisciplinary, their conversation was unspecialized, and involved translation from one mode of discourse to another. This kind of translation involves a neural translation, too, from one mode of mental processing to another, from right-brain geometrical insight to left-brain algebra, from left-brain wordplay to right-brain melodies and pictures, from cortical rational activity to frontolimbic passionate contemplation.

Now the transfer of ideas from one mental mode to another implies and perhaps brings into being a higher control function which is not of one or the other, but transcends them. It is closer to that "I," that inner self of inner selves which the Hindus call Atman, than any of the brain functions that it connects. The word *atman* has the same root as the Greek atmos, from which we get atmosphere; it literally means breath or air. So the word *spirit,* which comes from the Latin word for breath, is an exact translation. The essential characteristic of this interdisciplinary conversation, then, is that it is a spiritual one, in this sense of spiritual.

This idea is like Plato's notion of the value of mathematics in preparing a young mind for philosophy, as he explains it in the *Republic*. The philosopher, he says, deals with that which is true. That which is true cannot change; but all of our experience is of change. However, mathematics forces us to see behind the contingencies of particular instances and circumstances the eternal laws, such as the fact that two and two are equal to four, whether the entities added are apples, equal quantities of a substance, or people. Thus mathematics trains us to see the changeless behind change. Now we do not have to accept Plato's proposition that the truth is what is changeless to see the relevance of his idea to the immortal conversation. The interdisciplinary nature of the conversation will not allow an idea to remain in the specific field of expertise or setting of calculation or body of facts in which it was first propounded. It rises above the merely intellectual, the merely expert, the mere talent of its birth, and finds another life as carried or mediated by alternative incarnations. In this way the idea of the fulcrum balancing all against nothing recurs again and again in the School of Night, here as the algebraic method of bringing all of the terms of an equation over to one side and making them equal to nothing, there as the unbalanced composition of Nicholas Hilliard's extraordinary portrait of the Earl of Northumberland, here as Raleigh's giving the lie to the whole world, or weighing smoke for Queen Elizabeth, there as Hamlet's soliloquy, "To be or not to be."

So the heart of the immortality of the great conversation lies outside the conventional objects, skills, traditions, and expertise of discourse. It is not, as we said, merely immortality for the Great Minds; for it is precisely when these great minds give up being great minds—being experts, authorities, professionals—and become amateurs, laypersons—bullshitters if you like—that they begin to become immortal. It was the sophists who were the experts. Socrates and company jumped all the fences, like sophomores. They even jumped the sexual fence in some ways; and Socrates finds his best conversational partner, on the most important of all subjects, Love, in Diotima the wise woman of the *Symposium*.

And in Woolf's *To the Lighthouse* it is another wise woman, Mrs. Ramsay, who survives in some sense in the consciousness of her friends. Her wisdom is explicitly distinguished from the wisdom of the male intellectuals who gather at the house by the sea. It is the wisdom of a mother, which is already at that place at which the great male intellectuals arrive when they cast aside their expertise, their authority. For mothers are the ultimate interdisciplinarians, the ultimate amateurs, the ultimate laypersons. They are also the ultimate artists, in an art which is the hardest, most full of drudgery and care, of all: the creation and programming of new living human beings. How lucky it is for the men that they may now begin to share in that most truly immortal of activities! The writer who, driven by love for the uncreated poem, cannot sleep for its demands, is only a shadow of a Mrs. Ramsay:

> ...she quickly took her own shawl off and wound it round the skull, round and round and round, and then she came back to Cam (her daughter, who is afraid of the boar's skull on the wall) and laid her head almost flat on the pillow beside Cam's and said how lovely it looked now; how the fairies would love it; it was like a bird's nest; it was like a beautiful mountain such as she had seen abroad, with valleys and flowers and bells ringing and birds singing and little goats and antelopes...She could see the words echoing as she spoke them rhythmically in Cam's mind, and Cam was repeating after her how it was like a mountain, a bird's nest, a garden, and there were little antelopes, and her eyes were opening and shutting, and Mrs. Ramsay went on saying still more monotonously, and more rhythmically and more nonsensically, how she must shut her eyes and go to sleep and dream of mountains and valleys and stars falling and parrots and antelopes and gardens, and everything lovely, she said, raising her head very slowly and speaking more and more mechanically, until she sat upright and saw that Cam was asleep.

> Now, she whispered, crossing over to his bed, James must go to sleep too (James likes the boar's skull, of course), for see, she said, the boar's skull was still there; they had not touched it; they had done just what he wanted: it was there quite unhurt. (Op. cit., p. 172 et seq.; my parentheses)

This unbought and unpayable service cannot be demanded of any free human being; and so it is a good thing that motherhood and child care are no longer automatically expected of women. It is as if all men were expected to be great artists, and do it for nothing, and be condemned if they did not fully succeed! But motherhood and art must be free gifts, and their rewards must be free gifts. Our logic has led us to the conclusion that it is the amateurishness of the great minds that is closest to their immortality; and amateurs of course are not paid for their services, and do them as a free gift. We are faced with the apparently preposterous inference that those conversational circles where immortality has been seen historically to flourish achieve their transcendence of mortality by aspiring to the condition of mothers.

Now the immortality of mothers is essentially anonymous, in the sense that Virginia Woolf uses this word in *A Room of One's Own*—nameless, self-effacing. Even now the child still usually takes its father's name, and therefore the being of the mother in the child avoided the specificity and therefore the mortality of a name. The quality that makes a person desirous of giving herself or himself to another, and of printing one's being on another, and being imprinted with another's being, is love. Love is anonymous; it seeks only the good and higher happiness of the beloved. Now we have a sort of analogical explanation of the fact that those circles of immortal friends often did not bother to record their conversations. Anonymity is the final insurance against death.

Archeologists until recently gave us a picture of human prehistory which was almost entirely male-centered, not because they were chauvinists, but because the prehistoric men had entrusted their being to durable artifacts that can be dug up and displayed in a museum, or stand for many ages, like a pyramid. The women wove things, or sewed them in leather, or cultivated crops which do not leave hard bones for archeologists to find. A wiser paleoanthropology now tells us that the women were the culture-bearers, and they left a much more durable and complete legacy: us. Might not the durability of written wisdom be deceptive in some ways, like the archeological record? Is it not love that left a more lasting imprint, because it is an imprint that continues to change and grow? Might not the strangeness of poetry, its singsong, its assumption of a certain intimacy, its metaphorical and metrical transfers between different brain modes, be a kind of subversion of the text as bony relic, a resurrection of the rhythm of talk?

But it would be unwise to go too far in this direction, in our enthusiasm at having found a buried wisdom. The sense of immortality is almost strongest of all in tragedy, which explicitly concerns men who resist change heroically and who are destroyed by it but never surrender. Perhaps we can say this: that fully accepted and properly experienced suffering is good coin, and is valid in any exchange, even for love and self-surrender and growth, with all of which it has much in common. You see what a difficult task this is that we have set for ourselves, to dismiss neither the old male ethic of honorable consistency of being nor the new-old female ethic of wise cooperation and process. We must affirm both; to be partisans of the one is, quite unquestionably, to give up our own chance at immortality. As Woolf says in *A Room of One's Own*—as usual, doing exactly what she is saying—

> Coleridge perhaps meant this when he said that a grat mind is androgynous. It is when this fusion takes place that the mind is fully fertilized and uses all its faculties. Perhaps a mind that is purely masculine cannot create, any more than a mind that is purely feminine...(Virginia Woolf: *A Room of One's Own*, Harcourt Brace, New York, 1957, p. 102.)

If love and self-surrender and growth and accepted suffering are the medium of such immortality as we have, we find in them a sure defense against the charge that the Spiritus Mundi is an impersonal and morally irresponsible force that rapes the human individual or renders him or her into a terroristic instrument of historical destiny. If the Zeitgeist is made of love, it may be anonymous, but not impersonal. It is the disciplines, the specializations, the expertises that dominate, that enforce, that preserve the names of great men (and some great women). When one ventures out into the ocean of the interdisciplinary, where no track is left in the water, with one's good friends and shipmates in the enterprise—to use a core metaphor of *To the Lighthouse*—one should leave behind all attempts to enforce a mechanical immortality. The "I" that transcends any particular mode of mental processing is the most personal thing about me, even though, oddly enough, it is not my name or reputation or consciousness nor any of my skills or talents or expertises. It is that which *possesses* my name, my consciousness, my skills, and so on: and possession is a grand and sacramental connection, the basis of any incarnation, any communication, any real act in the world. It is partly constituted by those things, but it is not possessed by them.

If the Spiritus Mundi is love, it cannot be a coercive force, a rape. Love is not love if it is not free. We are not so much like neurons in a great brain, as like moments in a great sequence, states of a larger process, containing, holographically, a miniature and not totally enacted version of the whole.

And here we may approach an answer to the last objection: that memories and personal influences and ideas and even whole cultures are subject to temporal decay, and are only a little less transient than the human body itself.

At the end of *To the Lighthouse* Lily Briscoe is finally able to complete the picture she started while Mrs. Ramsay was still alive, the picture whose essential subject is the spirit of Mrs. Ramsay.

> There it was—her picture. Yes, with all its greens and blues, its lines running up and across, its attempt at something. It would be hung in the attics, she thought; it would be destroyed. But what did that matter? she asked herself, taking up her brush again. She looked at the steps; they were empty; she looked at her canvas; it was blurred. With a sudden intensity, as if she saw it clear for a second, she drew a line, there, in the centre. It was done; it was finished. Yes, she thought, laying down her brush in extreme fatigue, I have had my vision. (Op. cit., p. 309 et seq.)

The last obstacle that Lily must overcome is the thought that her commemoration of Mrs. Ramsay will be hung in attics. The overcoming of this feeling—"But what did that matter?"— is what enables her to complete her work. The implication is that the desire for immortality is the very thing that stands in the way of that vision which constitutes immortality. Suppose one can have had an experience, a vision, a communion, that one knows to be immortal. One is not having it now; and one quite explicitly will not have it again (the picture could be destroyed and it would not matter; repetition is simply not the point). Well then, is the process of the experience itself that which we feel to be immortal? Not quite; it is very important that Lily complete the picture, and lay down her brush. The product, the picture, is at least as important as the process by which it came into being—even though the picture may well have no future!

There is only one solution to the paradox, and that is that we have assumed a model of time which is not correct. Virginia Woolf's friend T. S. Eliot describes that moment of epiphany, that spot of time which carries the stamp of immortality, as "an intersection of the timeless with time." In *Four Quartets,* where this expression comes from, Eliot is bent on establishing a sacred religious realm whose milieu is that which intersects with time when we achieve those moments of enlightenment, of vision. Let us lay this explanation aside, for two reasons. One is that, as we have already seen, the desire for continuance or repetition itself can stand in the way of that utter giving which constitutes the vision. The other is that we are playing by Bloomsbury rules, remember, and must not assume the ineffable.

But Eliot's idea does suggest a sort of time-geometry that might fit our actual experience. When Lily says "I have had my vision" she is talking about an experience of immortality, but one which is already, if barely, in the past. The implication of this is that the immortality experience is, so to speak, at ninety degrees to the timeline of past-present-future as we usually conceive of it. Along the historical timeline we may pass through and out of that experience. But perhaps something in us changed course, and took off along that other axis; an axis for which the whole of ordinary historical time is only the starting-line, the zero point, the beginning of this new super-time.

Eliot is wrong, I think, in calling it timelessness; in doing so he is following in the great tradition of Plato and Augustine, who saw the world of the human experience of time as a corrupt and shadowy declension from the changeless perfection of eternity. That idea, beautiful as it is, is perhaps the best that men can do in the absence of women when it comes to defining the immortality experience. But the integrity of the experience demands an even greater yielding over of one's identity than the traditional male means—prayer, observance, alms, vows. When Jesus likened the kingdom of heaven to a mustard seed, or to growing wheat or leaven, or most of all to the perpetually stormy and dynamic experience of human love, he was not referring to anything outside of time. If anything, he is talking about an intenser form of time, one with more tenses, so to speak, not less. He is talking about something that does not stand still but grows, something that is here and now, not someplace else—like after we die, for instance. The kingdom of heaven is within, he said. Topologically "within" is the best preposition one could use for a direction which, like the six new dimensions of string theory in physics, takes off at ninety degrees to all three dimensions of space as well as to the timeline of past and future. The Upanishads, the sacred books of the Hindus, use similar language, and so does the wisdom of the Tao. Most animist and polytheistic religions never lost the sense of sacred time as being not less, but more, temporal than ordinary time. I am treating these sources not as authorities but as evidence; as if they were like those traditions of folk medicine which summarize generations of empirical wisdom, which are often wrong, but which, equally often, have come up with explanations and cures that modern medicine ignores at its peril. They may be more than this, but they are at least rather remarkably consistent records of human experience.

The best current thinking about time suggests that time itself evolved, from the directionless and disconnected time of quantum mechanics, through the irreversible, deterministic, and entropic world of classical physics and chemistry, into the purposive and constructive realm of life. We are as far beyond that realm, with our multiple futures, our freedom, and our complex tense-structure, as it is beyond its predecessors. Could it be that the immortality experience is the next, more advanced, intenser, more complex type of temporality, as it begins to come into being? Like Wittgenstein, who found himself forced to break the rules of discourse he was setting up in the very act of making those rules, and stating a boundary to consciousness which immediately ceases to be a boundary when it is stated, have we not, in the very attempt to avoid the ineffable, found out a new concept of time?

Let us in conclusion add this last, rather speculative and abstract note to our characterization of the Great Conversation. It may be that Dante and Blake were able to talk with the Old Testament prophets precisely because, along that other way or growthline of time, they were contemporaries.

Once one has experienced the living being of those past spirits, and found one's own voice in that glorious colloquy, one's own death takes on a different meaning. Wallace Stevens cannot be denied when he says that death is the mother of beauty; on that account one would not wish to be shortchanged of any of the finality of death. The mother, notice. Stevens also asks in the same poem: Is there no change of death in paradise? and we may now answer, No, there is death in paradise. Supposing this is true, then we are living in paradise right now, if we could only turn that corner and see the place for the first time. And it is our friendly discourse with each other, our talk of souls, say those wisest culture-bearers, that can help us turn the corner.

A FUTURE FOR EDUCATION

The last section turns to the practical cultural enactment in the academy of the ideas in this book. The first essay in this section demonstrates that the present organization of the university into departments falsifies the actual organization and shape of the universe. A single process of cosmic evolution left us a world which is the hierarchically nested, dynamic, and radically interconnected record of its own developmental history. Alternative strategies for academic organization are suggested and the new cybernetic technology evaluated as a means to implement them.

The second essay in this section proposes radical changes in the social disciplines, especially history and sociology, based on a critique of traditional historical, social, and economic determinism. New developments in chaos theory are used to suggest an epistemology and research practice based on modelling from partial information, and performative reenactment.

In the last essay the humane, celebratory, and deeply creative pedagogical methods of the anthropologist Victor W. Turner are explored in relation to my own teaching practices. They include a fundamental interdisciplinarity, a central performative and performance element, and a fully human and reflexive personal milieu, and exemplify a reunification of the ritual, artistic, and intellectual/ analytic approaches to reality.

8   *Beyond the Disciplines*

Design for a New Academy

Clearly something is missing in the way that we are educating our children. And despite our penchant for administrative and financial solutions, I believe we must look to the content of education—its conception of the shape of the world, and therefore its manner of introducing students to it—for both a diagnosis and a cure.

What is that missing something? Most fundamentally it is a sense of cognitive unity, a unity which imparts meaning to the world and from which our values unfold. We cannot go backward to look for this unity; but perhaps it lies before us if only we can cleanse the gates of our perception.

The great obstacle to our perception is the academic curriculum in its current shape. The last four hundred years of scientific and intellectual progress contain a gigantic paradox. Every great advance, every profound insight in the sciences and other intellectual disciplines, has torn down the barriers and distinctions between those disciplines; and yet the institutional result of each of these achievements has been the further fragmentation and specialization of the academy.

Let us consider the following list of disciplines: mathematics, physics, chemistry, biology, anthropology, the arts and humanities, theology. This list is not in random order; it represents roughly the sequence of prerequisites that one will usually find in a college catalog. That is, a theology major will usually be expected to take arts and humanities courses; an arts and humanities major will be encouraged to take something in anthropology; an anthropologist will surely be expected to take physical anthropology, which requires some knowledge of biology; a biologist must know some chemistry; a chemist must have a working understanding of physics; and a physicist is lost without mathematics. I believe that this sequence reveals

117

a certain instinctive wisdom in the academy, though its larger implications would be denied by many academics. This wisdom points toward a vertical, as opposed to horizontal, unity in the world, a unity which is implicitly denied by many of our fundamental academic metaphors—"field of study," "department," "the language of a specialty," even "discipline" itself. We need a new metaphor; what follows is a search for it.

The spirit of the academy has long been the spirit of specialization. Isaac Newton, the founder of modern physics, is often credited with the invention of the first specialized academic discipline. But Newton's greatest achievement was to unify mechanics, astronomy, algebra, geometry, and optics in such a way as to bridge the border between mathematics and physics, so that from his time forth there could be no physics that was not based on mathematics. Interestingly enough, this connection only goes one way; that is, it would not be accurate to say that there can be no mathematics which is not based on physics. The mathematics of physics, though the only mathematics which is actualized in space and time, is a limited sample of the total set of possible mathematical concepts and operations.

Let us consider another great scientific achievement: the reduction of chemistry to physical principles by such nineteenth-century scientists as John Dalton, whose *New System of Chemical Philosophy* may be as important as Newton's *Principia*. Chemistry could be no more than a series of isolated observations until the principles of atomic weight, specific heat, and chemical combination and valence had been established and, above all, until the periodic table of the elements had been drawn. But all of these discoveries were in essence a demonstration that chemistry is really a subset, or branch, of physics—that a chemist clinches any argument about his or her conclusions by demonstrating its derivation from known physical principles. Now, much of physics deals with a world in which chemistry need never have come into being, except insofar as chemistry is required to bring about physicists. Indeed, there is no chemistry over three thousand degrees centigrade, and because the universe is believed to have begun at a very much higher temperature than that, the laws of physics were sufficient to describe its operations until it cooled sufficiently to permit stable molecules to form. So both the logic and the history of chemistry describe it as a special case of physics, whereas there is no sense in which physics is a special case of chemistry.

But we need not stop here. One of the most decisive discoveries in biology was that of the double helix structure of the DNA molecule. From this point on, no biologist could be considered to have consolidated a conclusion until it could be demonstrated to be plausibly consistent with the biochemistry of life. In other words, biology is a huge branch of chemistry— biology is what chemistry does when given a volatile cesspool like the planet Earth and some billions of years to play around with. Again the relationship between the disciplines is asymmetrical: chemistry is not a branch of biology, and one could fairly say that the microstructure of biology is chemistry.

Consider now, anthropology—in its broadest sense, as including sociology, psychology, political science, economics, and all of the other human sciences. Just as the liveliest controversy once surrounded the reduction of biology to the interaction of dead matter (that is to say, chemistry), so now the most vigorous argument involves the extent to which the study of human beings is fundamentally the study of an animal species. A remarkable species we are, truly, say the pioneers of this view—as chemistry is a remarkable kind of physics and biology a remarkable kind of chemistry—but an animal species nevertheless. There is a massive convergence in process among the fields of paleoanthropology, sociobiology, human ethology (the study of human behavior as one kind of animal behavior), neurology, psychophysics, linguistics, genetic archaeology, and archeology, and this convergence points to the imminent collapse of the old boundary that separated the study of humankind from the study of the rest of nature. But again, the relationship—between biology and anthropology—will be one-sided. Biology is not a branch of anthropology, but it may well be that anthropology is a branch of biology, and that the microstructure of anthropology is biology.

The moment one says this in public, one is liable to lose a good section of one's audience; the Scopes trial is still being argued out, and the irony is that many of the opponents of the idea that the study of human beings is fundamentally the study of animals consider themselves enlightened defenders of liberty. We do not like being compared with animals; we believe that we are free and animals are not. But there is no reason to believe that our biological descent makes us automatons, any more than the other higher animals are. On the contrary; what other rational account of the appearance of novel entities in the world is there than evolution? And what is freedom but the ability to generate novel entities? As biological evolution produced that radical novelty known as humankind—as it had earlier produced the radical novelties of eukaryotes, vertebrates, and primates—so that enormously accelerated version of evolution which we call the human imagination is capable of the leap into a new world, the leap called freedom.

But we cannot stop even here. The same ferment that is seething at the border of biology and anthropology is going on at the border of anthropology and the arts, in such fields as cultural anthropology and folklore. And the result of this ferment will be the final recognition of the arts and humanities as a branch, or subset, of anthropology. So art history, literary criticism, and the rest will have to validate themselves—as chemistry validates itself physically, and as physics validates itself mathematically—by reference to sound anthropological knowledge.

Finally the time will come when the boundary between theology—the study of the divine—and the arts and humanities will be breached in the same way, and we shall evaluate and temper our religion on the basis of what our arts and humanities tell us about ourselves. We will come to see Dante, Shakespeare, Goethe, Nietzsche, Michelangelo, Mozart, and our own Emerson, Thoreau, Melville, and William James as prophets of such unity. When this time comes, Francis Bacon's and René Descartes's great split between the divine and the natural will have been healed, and we will be back on the main road of human cultural evolution.

In a certain limited sense, then, all academic disciplines are subbranches of mathematics. Perhaps we can put it another way: the laws of the world form a gigantic pyramid, with mathematics at the bottom layer, physics the next, and so on, and with the arts and theology at the top. To understand any layer profoundly, it is necessary to plunge into the discipline beneath it. This hierarchical structure is the dynamic residue of the actual process of evolution in its broadest sense: the evolution of coherent forms of energy out of the probabilistic chaos and mathematical constraints of the first nanoseconds of the Big Bang; the evolution of stable particles and then stable atomic structures as the universe cooled to the point where nuclei could retain electrons; the cooking up of the elements of the periodic table inside the cores of massive stars and the evolution of chemistry as local temperatures dropped below three thousand degrees; the evolution of life three and a half billion years ago; and the evolution of humankind in the last five million.

At each point in this development the universe leaped to new magnitudes of complexity and integrated organization. It would take an inconceivably greater number of bits of information to describe the current universe than to describe the universe of four billion years ago, and that universe would in turn take many more bits than the incandescent universe of the Big Bang. The further back we go, the fewer physical laws there were, and the simpler the universe. In a sense, the Big Bang universe is still with us as a kind of living fossil, exemplified in the probabilistic and indeterminate interactions of the smallest known physical particles. But at one time that was all there was, and there would have been no need for the laws of chemistry, biology, and so on.

The general structure of the hierarchy of the universe is now clear, and the great epoch of academic specialization and value-free experiment that revealed it might well be expected to be coming to an end. But something very peculiar happened to the academy. Even as the essential unity of the world was being revealed, the academy increasingly divided itself into smaller and smaller microfields and microdisciplines. One reason for this is that the sociology of scientific investigation has demanded an essentially democratic and antiauthoritarian context, and thus the hierarchical form of the organization of the universe has had to be denied lest the cognitive dissonance with the spirit of inquiry paralyze the research effort. Our political philosophy has not been sophisticated enough to reconcile a hierarchical universe with a democratic society.

Another reason for academic specialization is human limitations; nobody is capable of absorbing the whole content of human thought. But the error of the academy has been to deny, by means of its metaphors of demarcation between fields, the intimate connections, the continuous and omnipresent relevance of other fields at every stage of investigation. After all, the metaphorical implication of the phrase "another field"— "not my area," as academics say—is that the other field is over there, not right under one's feet. It would have been wiser—but there was no way of acquiring this wisdom except by going through the mistake—to describe the work of other scientists and scholars as being inside or containing one's own work, or as being above or below it. We would thus acknowledge the commonality of the world that we study, and the uncomfortable fact that, for instance, the arts and humanities are a more advanced, but less basic, area of study than physics. To put this in an even more radical way: the arts and humanities are higher physics.

The present model of the academy, implicit in the metaphor of the academic field or area, is of a vast flat plain stretching in all directions and divided by departmental fences into disciplines, each with its own rules, language, and canons of proof. If, on the other hand, the universe itself is much more like a pyramid, then the academy is running the grave risk of falsifying the universe by its model. After all, the most insidious kind of misinformation is the kind that is not explicit but conveyed by the very form of the inquiry. So it is essential that we change our basic metaphor.

Such a change of metaphor is not conceptually impossible. One way of thinking about the structure of the new academy is in terms of one's own body. We do not need to know in detail how the minute chemical servomechanisms of the muscles operate in order to move our arms, or how the visual cortex performs its staggering miracle of constructing a coherent visual world out of the buzzing, blooming confusion that hits the retina. But we do need to learn, as babies, how to operate the general controls that make it all work. Likewise, a detailed knowledge of the fields that underlie one's own discipline is not necessary, as long as we are able to understand their major principles and laws, their most powerful theoretical generalizations, and as long as we know where to look and what to use in order to retrieve more precise information as that becomes necessary.

So we need to teach our students in a "top-down" fashion how the grand principles work; and perhaps we should be prepared to abandon, sometimes, the minute processes of research by which we discovered those principles, at least until the student's general understanding is strong enough for him or her to ask intelligent questions. If the big principles really are as good as we believe, they will imply the minutiae of experimental and mathematical procedure, much as a motor command implies its implementation by the nervous system and muscles. If a student has a sound understanding of the principles of evolution, the beauty of the idea will encourage enough observation of nature to suggest how it was originally proved.

At this point an important distinction must be made. I am not advocating courses in research methods as such—"teaching students how to learn," as it is often termed. The brain is hungry not for method but for content, especially content which contains generalizations that are powerful, precise, and explicit. Our memories are addressed and referenced not by an abstract methodological grid but by significant fragments of their own content. Thus our core courses should deal first with the why of the world, not the how of research, because the how of research is generated by the why of the world.

This may all sound harmless enough; but beware. What I am suggesting is that we reverse our ordinary procedure of teaching—method first and conclusions afterward. Instead we must teach the conclusions first. When Bacon inaugurated the scientific project, it was indeed necessary to discard all of the classical conclusions about why the world worked the way it did, for they were not true in practice. Thus it was necessary to start off with method, and make that method as sure as possible in its exclusion of error. But we have been at this work for four hundred years, and the principles we have discovered work when we design an automobile, a telephone, a new strain of wheat. And those principles are more or less consistent with one another, and together can often act as a check on or confirmation of speculation based on one of them alone. Only when paradoxes arise do we need to go back to the old skeptical method.

And if a piece of the information pyramid is missing—say, a body of data about turbulence and laminar flow—we will simply be prompted to go out and collect it. (I choose this example because I believe that, in this case, that is exactly what happened.) The point is that if the pyramid of information did not exist, but rather information was just spread out as far as it would go, as in the "academic field" model, there would be nothing to tell us when information was missing. The recent explosion of work in folklore and the oral tradition has a similar origin, I believe: because anthropology had been brought close enough to the humanities to be seen in some way to underpin them, we suddenly noticed how little information we had to make the connection, and set out to obtain it. And we found to our surprise that very rich sources lay right under our noses.

For those at home in the pyramid, nothing human is alien;

indeed, nothing is alien. To say this is to predict the end of a whole cast of academic thought, that Brahmin prejudice which once wrote off other cultures as savage, and which now writes off our technological shopping mall culture as barbarian or worse. The true pyramid dweller does not deplore pop culture. He or she sees it as the raw material of great art. Technology is one of the performing arts by which new realities come into being. And it needs scriptwriters, composers, choreographers.

The pyramid of knowledge is not a static or fixed one. It is continuously growing. And its growth is at all levels, the low as well as the high, the high as well as the low. This picture of things is not reductionist. Though by evolution the low can give rise to the high, the simple to the complex, the relatively determined to the relatively free, nevertheless the high, the complex, and the free, once they exist, can take control of those levels of existence that preceded them. This is a model in which we do not evaluate a descendant or an effect by reference to its parent or cause; rather we evaluate the cause or parent by its fruits and progeny. By their fruits ye shall know them; and it is not that which goeth into a man that defileth him, but that which cometh out of him.

If my body is healthy, I can use it without thinking about individual muscles; only if I am building a new skill—a new control system—or rebuilding a damaged one should I think about the details of bodily motion. Indeed, an athlete must learn to forget the details of his or her training to achieve the instinctive sense of flow that characterizes a champion. Knowledge of scientific principles is like the possession of a motor skill. Because we have those beautiful, powerful, hard-won principles, or control algorithms—the inverse square law of gravitation; $E = mc^2$; the laws of chemical combination; the interplay of selection, mutation, and recombination in evolution; the relationship between brain chemistry and behavior; the three-second line in human poetry; the tripartite structure of ritual and dramatic performance—let us teach them all at once, not as composite lumps of evidence but as the natural modes of human action and perception. Our students should feel the fire packed into the atom, the inertia of the thrown stone, the stream eroding the valley, the field of flowers genetically drifting with a little assist from herbivores and climatic change, the sense of social attunement and insight brought about by ritual chant or dramatic performance. They should see the earth's spin toward sunlight, not the sun rising. Science teachers ought to be poets; it goes without saying that poets have to be scientists.

I am not suggesting that we can give up the painstaking process of careful experiment in scientific research. The obsessed and dedicated experimentalist will always be necessary. The point that I am making is that there is now not only a process and method of science but also an achieved and powerful content—a content which must be grasped in principle by most citizens if we are to survive, and to survive as a democratic society.

What Prospero meant by Art—the unity of science, art, technology, moral choice, magic, craft, and delightful stage illusion—is increasingly feasible. Until recently, to demand such a vision of the academy was to demand too much. We teachers are mortal in our limitations, in our tendency to imitate the lower animals and safely specialize, in our plain incapacity to carry the enormous load of information that would make the vision concrete and meaningful to us—and therefore communicable—and in our passivity with respect to what we do know, our inability to put it to work, to extrapolate, to make models from it that can predict and make sense of the world.

What do human beings do when they encounter a task too great for their powers? They use tools, prostheses to bridge over the regions of weakness and thus connect and enable the regions of strength. Such tools are more various in their nature than we sometimes imagine. They include those prosthetic enzymes, the ferments, yeasts, and molds by which we eke out the weaknesses of our digestive systems and to which we owe our bread, our cheese, our wine; also the rules of our art forms, such as counterpoint, perspective, and meter, by which we amplify and extend the integrative powers of our minds; and of course those more familiar tools, like automobiles, violins, communications satellites, garden hoses, and hiking boots, by which we assist our muscles.

For centuries the most potent tool that teachers possessed was books; and indeed a book with an index and a margin for notes is a formidably compact, cheap, and powerful tool, of great elegance and simplicity, and in many ways superbly adapted to the human brain and body. But printed books were themselves the answer to a crisis in information processing, a crisis that historians call the rise of the middle class. They were invented as prostheses to supplement the marvelous but finally inadequate information processing system of the middle ages, which combined script and icon with various psychic technologies, such as narrative, meter, rhetoric, drama, the disputation, and the associative memory systems.

Today the sheer numbers of books, their uncorrectability, and their linear, stereotyped, and deterministic form, have in turn rendered them incapable of handling on their own the integrative demands of the enormous information flow that they themselves helped to create. A new tool offers itself to the academy: the computer. Can it help?

Before we go any further it is vital to point out that new information processing tools do not necessarily extinguish old ones. The fundamental psychic technologies—story, meter, musical tonality, and so on—can never be rendered obsolete, being as they are the most effective channels of communication or interfaces with the human brain. Though the "memory-theater" of the medieval and renaissance mnemonic systems was effectively replaced by print, most of the other information processing systems are still very much alive, and may even be stronger than ever if we take into account the much larger proportion of the population that has access to them. It is significant that the greatest drama of all, that of William Shakespeare, was composed at the very moment of the triumph of the printed book; for drama is an ancient oral-audial psychic technology, essentially independent of print. By the same token we might well expect that the greatest glory of the book as a work of art still lies in the future, once the electronic media and the computer hve taken from it the baser burdens it must bear today.

So we must see the computer as in partnership with, even amplifying, the older information technologies. What can it bring to the partnership?

First, of course, the compact storage and easy retrievability of huge databases. With compact disk storage the computer now far surpasses the book in this respect; and the book was until now the most efficient information storage and retrieval device. More important, a computer database is not limited to a single index, but can construct a new index entry to the precise requirements of the reader in a fraction of a second. Related to this feature is the infinite correctability of computer data, and the infinitely wide "margin" for notes and comments that it offers. Books are much more limited in this respect; computer text is live text, like the lyrics of a folk ballad or oral epic. The fixity of book text requires a sharp division between the easy creative flow and messy approximateness of the rehearsal, the sketch, the rough draft on the one hand, and the lifeless finality of the finished version on the other. In the computer this division vanishes; each new version is the final version.

The computer can organize information as it is organized in the real world, that is, in the dynamic, branched, multidimensional hierarchy of hypertext. In this respect computer information is more like pictorial than printed information, but without the limitation to two dimensions (plus one for the "stretched" picture, in perspective). Music, discourse, oratory, and book text are all forced to spin out their information into a single one-dimensional linear thread. This computer text echoes in its shape and format the new hierarchical form of the universe as it comes clearly into view.

One consequence of this last feature is that computer information is, so to speak, free. At each of the branch points of the information tree there is a choice, and the correctability of computer text (together with its formidable capacity to readjust the whole system to one change, as in the spreadsheet or word processor index function) makes it possible to originate new branch points and new branches anywhere.

Given this "branchiness," computer information can closely model the interdisciplinary nature of the real world. It is not disorganized, as book text tends to be, by digression; and what is digression but the very principle of order, subordination, control, and freedom in real physical systems? Each branch of a tree is a fertile digression. A book must stick to its subject, and therefore carefully fenced off "subject areas" must be defined. A computer program can store under any entry a whole world of subordinate information, which may belong to another discipline altogether in the old dispensation. The footnote is but a clumsy approximation to this ability.

"Branchiness" in turn makes possible the interactive character of computer information. The reader is always also a writer, a participant observer. In this respect the computer mode takes a great leap backwards, to the interactiveness of oral modes of information processing, without losing the accuracy, stability, and immortality of book text.

The interactiveness of computer information fosters a closer bond between the text and the endorphin and enkephalin reward of the human brain. The brain rewards itself for a completed cycle of action and feedback. Literature—poetry, stories, and so on—is a way of making book text interactive so as to activate this reward system, but it takes an artistic knack and training to fold most types of information down into such springy forms as will maintain a conversation with a reader. In a sense the computer can make such interaction a routine feature; and this may explain the curious addictiveness of the activity of computer programming. It is as if we were getting the normal brain reward for work that the microprocessor has done.

Out of these features comes another: the ability of the computer to generate alternate scenarios or world models, based on different variables. Now it is this activity that the human brain is supremely good at, and that constitutes our odd unspecialized specialization as animals. Compared with our own fantastic power and subtlety in this regard—consider the astonishing reality, force, and hidden wisdom in a really good dream, for instance—a computer's skills are crude and clumsy. But we have never before had such help as it can offer. In the realm of the numerical, especially the iterative and the recursive, where the result of an equation can be fed back into the equation a million times over, and then represented visually in the exquisite patterns of the Mandelbrot Set or Conway's game, the computer offers to us a whole new set of senses. This dynamic reflexiveness may be the most remarkable capacity that the computer can give to the academy.

Our internal world models, as I hinted earlier, are no longer as irrelevant to reality as they seemed under the worldview of nineteenth-century determinism. How we interpret the world depends on our available models of it; and the world itself gives different answers according to the different world-models behind the questions we ask of it. If our model is a universe of particles, it gives us particle answers; if our model is a wave universe, it gives us waves. The worlds of mind and matter are not divided; and the computer, as a mental prosthesis and as a modeling tool, is both an example and a facilitator of their essential unity.

Finally, the computer offers a connection with one of the great adventures of the human mind and imagination: the cration of artificial intelligence. I believe the goal of that enterprise to be possible, but oddly unimportant compared with the intellectual riches that will fall out from the process of its realization. After all, a man and a woman can in a matter of a few pleasant minutes construct a brand-new chemical computer of enormous—indeed superfluous—power almost any time that they want, if they are prepared for the years of programming it will require. But to trace a different path to intelligence!— imagine the wisdom and insight that would lead out of us. "To lead out:" if we translate that phrase literally into Latin, we get "educate."

A person educated in this way would be in a position to recover that sacramental sense of unity and meaning of the world which was lost when we took the great detour into academic specialization, and which utopians have since sought to impose, unsuccessfully and often bloodily, by political or economic force. Such a person would not be overwhelmed or paralyzed by the complexity of modern life, any more than we are overwhelmed by the complexity of our own nervous, motor, and sensory systems. We are plugged into our nervous system in such a way that we sit at the top of a long chain of delegated responsibility. We are at the console of the ultimate user-friendly computer, insulated from the literalism of the machine language by a hierarchy of richer and more powerful special languages designed for easy use and referenced by the most simple mental "mouse"—the transfer of attention.

Notice that in this speculative meditation on the educational system of the future the distinction between knowing and doing —between the sensory and the motor capacities—has been blurred. For information, once it is organized in the new great chain of being advocated here, will become instrumental and dynamic, pointing not only to other information but to action suggested by the value system implicit in its hierarchical organization. Performance, including technological invention and artistic creation, will become central to education at all levels.

Our educational system has had a dangerous predilection for reductionism—an addiction to the primary, the elementary. If, in love with the exactness of those entities that can exist at a primitive level, we dismiss as unreal anything that requires a more sophisticated temporal environment—values, for instance, or individuality, or freedom—we are seeking to turn back the evolution of the universe. We democratize the universe, so to speak, and thus reduce it to easy comprehensibility, avoiding the whole exhausting business of making value judgments by denying their validity. The hierarchical pyramid model, on the other hand, automatically provides the universe with distinctions of value. The evolutionarily later always subsumes and includes the evolutionarily earlier; and therefore, given any measure of value, the more advanced is going to possess more of it than the more primitive.

And it is precisely values that our educational system lacks. The work of the new academy will be to get those sweet and potent brain chemicals flowing, those endorphins which are apparently associated with our enjoyment of the higher intellectual, moral, and esthetic values. Only in an academy that makes clear the relative importance of things can such a priming of the pump of self-reward be coherently undertaken. And it is not just the higher values that will benefit from such teaching. The lower values have their rightful and honored place in such a hierarchy. In the value-flat model, there are no values at all, because there are no distinctions of values.

This is a call for a change in the fundamental paradigms of study, and in the nature and function of the academy itself—a change as great, perhaps, as that which marked the end of medieval scholasticism and the beginning of the Renaissance humanist university. We have in our own time a project that requires a full mutual engagement of all fields of study, physics as well as poetry, and the hint of a warrant for its success. And if not now, when?

9 A New Logic of Human Studies

Consider the following paradoxes. A welfare system designed by well-meaning politicians guided by the advice of the wisest sociologists and economists available, costing billions of dollars, whose net effect is to radically increase the numbers of the poor, especially women and children, and to deepen their misery, incapacity, and despair. A stock market that rises because the statistical instruments designed to detect similarities with previous rises are causing investors to make it rise in the same pattern; that helps to generate the financial conditions it predicts; and that crashes because it thinks it is about to crash. A social polity expressly created to ensure the equality of all citizens, that produces an archipelago of concentration camps across a continent; and whose theoretical dismissal of the concrete effectuality of theorizing unleashes real social forces of unparalleled savagry. A foreign policy that depends for its effectiveness on the fact that the government does not know it is being carried out. An economy that attracts foreign investment by borrowing so much money that it is able to remain politically stable and thus economically healthy.

More and more of our collective life seems now to be populated with such logical monsters, such scyllas and charybdises of reflection and feedback. Yet good as well as evil can be compounded by the peculiar kind of interest which they offer; unfairly, unto him who has much, much shall be given, and the kingdom of heaven is like a mustard seed.

But these monstrosities are the despair of any "scientific" sociology or historiography. And now physics itself, and even that purest sanctum of linear logic, mathematics, seems to have caught the plague. Those positive knowledges to which modernist history and sociology appealed for a model now seem almost as messy and chaotic as the seething life of human culture.

This new vision of the "positive sciences" has emerged from the brilliant recent studies of chaotic, nondeterministic, recursive, fractal, dissipative, catastrophic, period-doubling, and feedback-governed systems, associated with the names of Mitchell Feigenbaum, Ilya Prigogine, Benoit Mandelbrot, and Rene Thom. Perhaps some of the terms of this new science require a brief (and necessarily incomplete) explanation. An algorithm is a mathematical method for doing something—say, generating a geometrical shape in a computer graphic. A *recursive* algorithm is one that possesses an internal loop, such that the solution arrived at by one passage through the loop is fed back again into the beginning of the loop, "adding," as Benoit Mandelbrot puts it, "fresh detail to what has been drawn on previous runs." Mandelbrot gave the name *fractals* to a family of shapes, irregular and fragmented surfaces, curves, and "dusts," generated by recursive algorithms based on a random or arbitrary numerical "seed." These shapes are often self-similar, that is, they repeat their own form or type of form at different scales of magnification, so as to pack into their details at one scale a microcosm of the next larger scale. The space-filling curves of Peano are only one example. Mandelbrot sees these forms everywhere in nature; in trees, cloudscapes, coastlines, the bronchi of the lungs, corals, star clusters, waves, craters, and so on. A *dissipative* system is one that maintains its form not despite its tendency to decay but by means of it. Dissipative systems can be self-organizing; I shall discuss some examples later, such as certain forms of turbulence. The term is Prigogine's. A *catastrophe* is a discontinuity, as when the gradual increase of some factor suddenly crosses a threshold in which some entirely different state is precipitated; it can be observed when a cooling supersaturated solution suddenly crystallizes, or when an animal's behavior suddenly changes during a gradual change in the stress it is undergoing, or when a gradual change in economic factors triggers a massive move in the stock market index. René Thom was for the first time able to describe such discontinuities or catastrophes mathematically, in his catastrophe graphs. One version of them that occurs in physical systems is known as bifurcation. *Period doubling*— Feigenbaum's term—is what happens when certain ordered systems break up into chaotic ones, like a smoke-ring dissolving in the air; out of such chaotic situations, however, new forms of order can arise spontaneously given the right circumstances. Those new forms of order are drawn into being by a strange attractor, that is, a complex pattern implicit in the feedback situation itself.

The lawfulness governing such systems is of a radically different kind from the rules that govern classical deterministic systems, and that are embodied in the empirical causal logic of the modern scholarly humanistic disciplines. In other words, if even the sciences themselves no longer insist on a linear causal mechanism for events (and its attendant rules of objective and positivistic empirical evidence), then it is high time that the social, historical, and humane studies reevaluated their scholarly methods. The indeterminacy of quantum physics was hard enough for the academy to swallow. The new indeterminacy is of quite a different kind.

What the new science shows us is that the operation of fairly simple processes—the period-doubling mechanism of turbulence, for instance, or the random walk of particles precipitating to a crystal—can very rapidly bring about states of a system that are utterly unpredictable from their initial conditions. In a computer simulation of planetary orbits, for instance, there is an unstable zone in which the velocity and proximity of a satellite with respect to its primary is critical to whether it will settle into a stable orbit, whether it will escape altogether, or whether it will adopt an eccentric, continually changing looping orbit around its primary. Each time the initial velocity or position is defined to a further decimal place, the resultant orbit is radically different—not different so as to form a convergent series homing in on an asymptote, but utterly and unpredictably different. Thus the accuracy by which the world is defined makes a total difference to the nature of the world itself. A seacoast measured with a one-mile ruler might be hundreds of miles long; if measured by a foot-ruler, thousands; if by a micron ruler, millions; and each level of magnitude has its own lawfulness and predicts its own pattern of wave action as the surf rolls in.

Given their unpredictability, one might expect such processes to bring about mere chaos, mere ugly inchoateness. But no. Often enough they resolve themselves into extremely beautiful, complex, and stable structures, to which I give the generic term "paisleys." Such forms are coming to replace the classical shapes of ideal geometry—lines, triangles, circles, regular solids—as the governing imagery of the scientific visual imagination. Examples range from the convection cells of a good rolling boil in a teakettle or the planetary pattern of trade winds or Jupiter's Great Red Spot—a storm that has raged for hundreds of years—to the forms of electrical discharge, crystals, river drainage systems, and organic structures. These systems forget their causes, and indeed if their causal determination were the only language in which they could be understood, they would be inherently unintelligible. The "modeling" or "generative" logic by which they *are* now understood is profoundly new as a mathematical formalism, but, as I hope to show, very ancient as an intuitive human activity.

The test of whether we truly understand such a system is no longer our ability to predict it, but our ability to construct another system that does the same sort of thing as the original. Perhaps we could say that we still test by prediction, but what we are predicting is not a certain future state of the system but the general type of behavior of the whole system itself. In other words, we are predicting not along a line of time, but across a sort of plane. And this notion, of other temporal geometries than the linear, has enormous implications not only for the study of history, but for the arts, humanities, and social sciences in general.

The common feature in all of these systems is feedback. The simplest forms of feedback are given in the initial conditions, for instance the setting of the thermostat of a home heating furnace. In this case the only unpredictable element is the precise value of some parameter—in our example, the temperature of the house at a specific time, in the course of its wanderings up and down around the "attractor" or average temperature we have set for it. More complex feedback systems can set their own parameters, or even create the sort of parameters toward which they aspire or around which they oscillate. That is, their state at any given moment is the resultant of ordering processes that have arisen within the system itself.

Now the supreme example of such self-organizing systems is life. And we may go further and say that the evolution of life has been the evolution of more and more autonomous and complex and unpredictable—because inventive—feedback systems. The human species is, as far as we know, the most advanced state of this process, where it shows in its most paradigmatic and articulated form the general tendency it always exhibited. Nature strives toward freedom, in the sense of autonomy, as the clearest expression of its essence. And here of course we return to our subject, which is the present crisis in history and social studies.

For surely, *a fortiori,* the collective activities of human beings are of all phenomena in the world the most fully governed by the principles of complex feedback systems. Social game theory takes us part of the way. Consider a simple dyadic predicting contest: a little marital spat on a Sunday in some large American city. There is tension between Jack and Jill; they haven't been able to talk much recently, because they have both been working hard. Jack, as usual, intends to get Sunday lunch. Jill, however, knowing what Jack has in mind, intends to shop for lunch at the deli instead, in order to upset him. But Jack knows his Jill. Guessing that she intends to go out to the deli in order to forestall Jack's usual lunch, Jack plans to claim that he is feeling ill and doesn't want lunch. Jill, though, expects the "I feel sick" ploy, and finds occasion to joke pleasantly about Jack's past propensity to use pretended illness to get out of things. Jack, recognizing that the game has got too complex at this level, changes levels by deliberately randomizing his own behavior. He starts a tedious conversation about fatal illnesses. Jill is flummoxed only for a moment; then recognizes the paradigm- or genre-switch. She plays the same game, but without any pretence at normal conversation, breaking in with some earnest remarks about chickadee nesting habits. She has thus thematized the issue of avoiding the subject and changed the ground rules once again. Jack now steps outside of the conversation and looks at it as a stranger might; no longer as "Jack versus Jill" but as "Jack and Jill versus the outside world." He sees how absurd they sound, catches Jill's eye, and they both collapse in laughter. No doubt they will go out to lunch at their favorite cafe. Or maybe not.

Jack and Jill have become a "we" by internally modelling each other's motivations and each other's image of the other. In the process they have touched on a broad and sensitive range of values and value judgments. Their story is not atypical; the narrative and dramatic arts are full of this sort of thing, and Erving Goffman and Thomas Scheff, among others, have provided close analyses of it. Now imagine it extended to the billions of dyadic relationships in the human world, and the trillions of larger group relationships. Nor are such strategies unique to intimate relationships. One could easily demonstrate the same sort of strategy at work between, say, two opposing generals in the wars of the Austrian Succession. All human interactions significantly involve such halls of mirrors.

Our first observation, that it was an error to apply to human

affairs the deterministic logic of classical science, would, if left
on its own, imply that we might as well give up on such studies
altogether. But there is now a body of theory and concept that
can put them on a new footing. In the remarks that follow I
pay special attention to historical and social studies, but I do
so to let part stand for whole; much of what I have to say
applies broadly to the humanities, the academic study of the
arts, and the human sciences as well.

For want of a nail, the kingdom was lost. The eddy in the
air caused by a butterfly in Brazil can amplify itself into a
dust devil, a whirlwind, a tropical storm, and finally a hurri-
cane that ravages Florida. Imagine the predicament of an
historian, reminded, by some trivial historical episode with
momentous effects, of the insecurity of the discipline of history.
The tiniest event can snowball into the most gigantic consequences, just as the minutest subatomic difference in a flow
can result in an utterly altered pattern of turbulence. Philosophers of history have never been able to demonstrate that
this snowball effect *cannot* take place. Perhaps every event
that occurs is just as crucial, and just as insignificant, because
it is undifferentiated in importance from everything else. Perhaps this is the spectre, the existential cackle of empty laughter, that haunts certain historians, that drives them to construct their elaborate deterministic edifices of economic and
social history, class struggle, invisible oppressors, conspiracy
theories. Like Casaubon in *Middlemarch,* they set out to
uncover the Key To All The Mythologies.

Another kind of historian with a different temperament, confronted with the appalling indifference of historical significance, will seek to enumerate all of the primary sources, to
recite all of the "facts," to deal with all exceptions to all rules,
all special cases, all of the statistics, and to do it without bias,
without giving any one fact more significance than any other.
It is as if one should seek an understanding of a turbulent flow
by listing and mapping all of the positions of all of the particles
in the flow at all times. Perhaps if the map is on a fine enough
scale, the answer will emerge. The mapmakers of Borges's mad
dictator who made a map of the country so perfect that when
opened it covered the country itself and brought on its economic ruin, or the mole in Kafka's story who kept building
new tunnels to keep watch on the entrances of his burrow, are
literary examples of the mindset. Such heroic historians, fixated
on the old intellectual modes, accumulate a tragically meaning-

less scholarship. Given this approach, why should not a life of scholarship that devoted itself to a descriptive catalog of every spot on the library wall—and there are enough spots on any library wall, if we choose small enough parameters—why should not such a labor be just as valid as Darwin's collection of evidence for evolution, or Albert Lord's for oral composition? Why is one fact more significant than another?

Not unlike the collecting moles in their theory, but different from them in practice, are those deconstructive postmodernists who accept the complexity and interdependence of the world, but refuse to recognize the real stable order that it also generates. Unable to escape their own oedipal and patriarchal model of knowledge, which insists that the identity of something derives from what originated it, they regard order as an illusion because that order originated out of chaos. Self-made men and women, they are as horrified by the idea of the self-made—by the *made*—as by the primal scene itself. For them to make, to create, is a fascist imposition of a totalizing structure upon the free play of the world. They thus abolish the idea of the writer, the maker, the text, the made thing, even the reader, even the world. They seize on quantum theory as a sort of warrant for a deconstructed and valueless universe—quite erroneously, of course, as indeterminate particles happily clump together to make very determinate pieces of matter. That those determinate pieces of matter in turn evolved sometimes into self-ordering and even free systems does not help the deconstructionists' case.

If the responses of the historical determinists, the obsessive collectors, and the rebels without a cause are inadequate to the problem of history, what approach might really work? The beginnings of an answer to this question are what this essay proposes; to get there we must follow a somewhat winding path of dialectical reasoning.

Any analysis of historical events that we make, or any theory of social behavior that we formulate, is itself one of the determining factors in the situation it describes. Thus there is no "meta" position, no detached Olympian viewpoint from which objective assessments can be made, and therefore no escape from the apparent chaos of mutual feedback. We are all revolutionaries and reactionaries, whatever our claims as historians or social scientists. Economists are just another group of competitors over what constitutes value.

Not that this struggle for ontological control is a blind one.

We would be totally ineffective at it if we were not able to assess the motives and assume the worldview of others. And even this would not be enough. Our imaginative model of the other must contain its own image of oneself; and that image itself must contain its own assessment of the other. And our outer negotiations take place not just between our own persons but also among the entire *dramatis personae* of the inner drama by which we estimate the future. The confusion is not one of blindness, but of too much sight; not of randomness, but an excess of determinants; not of chaos, but of an order too complex to be explained before the next complicating event comes along—of which the next, complicating, event *is* the best explanation.

Indeed, this capacity to impose our interpretations on things is not only our predicament but also what enabled us to second-guess, predict, and control the simpler systems of nature, such as the biological, chemical, and physical ones. We bought our power over the rest of nature with the essential uncontrollability of human events. We can control nature to the extent that we stay one step of reflexivity ahead of it. Nor is even nature innocent, but is itself the resultant and living history of a cosmic evolution which pitted many forms of reflection against each other; the marvellous cooperation of nature is a prudent and subtle form of mutual feedback. Even so, when we find that we can reduce another organism to a successfully testable set of laws and predictions, it is a sign that we are dealing with a lower order of reflection than our own.

Thus to attempt to do so with human beings—to educe and apply the laws governing them and to predict their actions—is, in human terms, a viciously aggressive act, an attempt to get control at the expense of others' freedom. It implicitly reduces human beings to the level of lower animals, even to that of inanimate things. But this indeed is what much social and economic history, much sociology and progressive political theory, have attempted to do. The promise such studies held out was not lost on those with the sweet thirst for power. Transformed into political programs those systems appeared in our century as the great totalizing regimes—Marxism, Fascism, National Socialism, International Socialism. We should not be surprised at the vigorous counterreaction of human culture against such systems.

In the light of this analysis it now becomes clear why, with the best will in the world, all principled revolutions have ended up diminishing human variety and freedom in their societies. For a revolution to be truly freeing it must be unprincipled, in the sense that its intentions do not rest on a predictive theory of human social behavior. Principles in this sense must be sharply distinguished from *values,* which are much more complex products and guides of human history, including within them the nonlinear flexibility and creativity of their past. The American Revolution was an unprincipled revolution, which is why it succeeded when so many failed. But unlike many later revolutions it did not question the great values of human life, and indeed recommitted itself to them. Such principles as the American Revolution possessed, enshrined in the Constitution, really amount to a declaration of regulated intellectual anarchy or unprincipledness. The separation of powers, which is, more than equality and even more than democracy, the central message of the Constitution and the thematic undertone of every article, is an intuitive recognition of the reflexive, self-organizing, unpredictable, feedback nature of history, which by reinterpreting its initial conditions is able to forget them.

Separation of powers makes politics into a drama, not a treatise. Perhaps the true hidden presence behind the Constitution is William Shakespare. All the world's a stage. We are all actors, in both senses of the word. Our inherent value derives from that condition, not from Kant's notion that we are ends in ourselves. We can still keep our dignity even if we are, for the time being, only means, as long as we are actors in the drama. Even if their function is to serve, the crusty boatman or witty nurse or pushy saleslady are interpreting the world from their own center, are characters, *dramatis personae,* to be ignored by others at their peril; and are thus free. We might parenthetically, therefore, view with alarm the tendency in modern and deconstructive postmodern theater to get rid of characters altogether.

But of course even *this* formulation that I have made is itself a part of the situation it describes; it is a speech in the play, to be evaluated by your own reflexive processes of assessment. Let us see whether the line of thought it prompts is a more or less freeing one than its competitors.

We immediately run up against a large problem. Does this critique of historical and human studies mean that they must revert to the status of chronicle and appreciative observation? Like amateur naturalists, must their practitioners only be collectors, without testable hypotheses or laws? Should we just admire the exquisite coiled turbulence of human events, wonder, and move on? The French historian Fernand Braudel is almost such a historical naturalist; there are moments as one contemplates his great colorful, slowly roiling paisley of Mediterranean history, seemingly without direction or progress, that one could wish for little more out of history. Should not the historian be a sort of Giovanni Casanova, a picaro among the courts and sewers of eternal Europe or China, remarking the choice beauties to be seen on one's travels?

A directionless view of history can be seductive. But even if the essential logic of the modern humane disciplines is utterly erroneous, it has nevertheless provided an impetus and direction for research, and has led to the vigorous discovery of huge masses of information, at least some of which is interesting to everyone. The bias of that information, the preponderance of certain types of sources, and the direction of the researchers' gaze may be corrupting; but in itself we feel the information to be valuable.

But let us explore the possible utility of the naturalist's or chronicler's agnosticism. Although it might not wish to own up to it, deconstructionism actually presents a rather good case for this perspective; to the extent that a case as such, with all its theoretical baggage, can be made for so uncaselike an approach. Deconstruction is purposely not long on logic, and as such it is quite consistent. The bête noire of all deconstructionists is totalization. What does totalization mean? Once we have disposed of those cases of totalization that every sane person would deplore—Nazism, for example—we get into interesting territory. What makes deconstruction unique is its inability to distinguish between those forms of order we would all agree are evil, and such things as marriage and family, the narrative structure of a text, the idea of the writer and the reader, and even the very idea of the self or person. There is no plausible place for deconstructionists to stop on their slide into total inarticulacy. Poor Jacques Derrida, nailed recently to the wall on the subject of South Africa, was forced to squirm to reconcile the indifference of his skepticism toward all forms of order, his fundamental belief in the radical apartheid of all points of view, and his decent liberal distaste for the regime.*

Certainly History and Sociology would be easy meat for a deconstructionist's acid test; but so would any human or indeed natural product, process, or action. Deconstructionism has now begun to turn its acids on itself; as it does so, it will encounter the paradox of what container to keep the perfect corrosive in. And if it is not the perfect corrosive, deconstruction must end up, like its old enemy Descartes, asserting with more totalizing violence than any other system the one idea that is not subject to the deconstructive process. In Descartes's system, it is the *cogito, ergo sum,* "I think, therefore I am," isolated by his skepticism about all else. In Derrida's, it is that force or energy that he perceives as prior to and underlying all difference.

But there is a rather benign face to deconstructionism, to be found for instance in Jean-Francois Lyotard's classic essay on postmodernism. It offers a way of thinking about human society that makes no generalizations and that recognizes all human activities and thoughts as flows in a great interacting soup of information. On the face of it, a very attractive vision; and it satisfies some of the criticisms we levelled earlier at History and the Social "Sciences."

But in doing so it abdicates that very activity—holistic understanding and the enrichment of the world by interpretation—that characterizes the human *Umwelt,* the human species-world, itself. The admonition not to totalize is the most totalitarian command of all, because it essentially dehumanizes history. The feedback process of human culture is a feedback *of* what deconstructionists would call totalizations. The open-endedness of history is created by the competition and accommodation of various candidates for the last word, the *dernier cri,* the formula of closure (including this one); it is an ecology of absolutisms. Nor is this ecology a random play of flows, without direction or growth; technology, records, and enduring

---

*Jacques Darrida, "Racism's Last Word," *Critical Inquiry,* 12, 1985; Anne McClintock and Rob Nixon, "No Names Apart: the Separation of Word and History in Derrida's "Le Dernier Mot du Racism," *Critical Inquiry,* 13, 1986; Jacques Derrida, "But, Beyond..." (Open letter to Anne McClintock and Rob Nixon, same issue of *Critical Inquiry);* Alexander Argyros, "Prescriptive Deconstruction," *Critical Texts,* forthcoming.

works of art constitute ratchets which prevent any return to earlier, less complex states of the system, just as genetic inheritance did in earlier ages. Thus history is an evolutionary system, with the three factors required for evolution to take place: variation (provided by the unpredictable paisley of reflexive events), selection (provided by the competition and accommodation of "totalizations"), and inheritance, a conservative ratchet to prevent what is of advantage from being lost.

The only way open is to seek forms of understanding and descriptive categories that are proper to our own level of reflexive complexity. To do this is essentially an artistic, a constructive, a performative, a religious activity, and it cannot fully depend on the capacity for calculation by which we claim to understand the rest of the natural world. (Even this claim must yield at a certain point. Ultimately scientists appeal to the beauty of a theory to justify it before the infinite plenum of its equally consistent rivals.) History is an art, even a technology, even a liturgy, as much as it is a science; and it is so not only in the activity of historiography, but also in that of research.

I am proposing, in other words, a change in our fundamental paradigm of historical and human study. And here another set of major scientific advances comes into play. Most workers in the historical and sociological fields still accept the cultural determinism that was one of the first naive responses of the West to the cultural diversity of the newly discovered nonwestern world. Thus for them the units of historical study, human beings, are *tabulae rasae,* blank sheets to be inscribed by cultural conditioning or economic pressures.

More recently, however, in fields as diverse as cultural anthropology, linguistics, twin-studies, paleoanthropology, human evolution, psychophysics, performance studies, neuroanatomy, neurochemistry, folklore and mythology, and ethology, it is becoming clear that we human beings bring to history and society an enormously rich set of innate capacities, tendencies, and exclusive potentials. We uncannily choose, again and again, the same kinds of poetic meters, kinship classifications, calendars, myths, funerals, stories, decorative patterns, musical scales, performance traditions, rituals, food preparation concepts, grammars, and symbolisms. We are not natureless. Indeed, our natures include, genetically, much of the cultural experience of our species in that period of one to five million years of nature-culture overlap during which our biological evolution had not ceased, while our cultural evolution had already begun: the period in which we unwittingly domesticated and bred ourselves into our humanity. The shape and chemistry of our brains is in part a cultural artifact. We are deeply written and inscribed already, we have our own characters, so to speak, when we come from the womb.

Having taken away one kind of rationality from historical and human studies, we may be able to replace it with another. But in so doing are we not committing the very sin, of reducing a self-organizing and unpredictable order to a set of deterministic laws, of which we accuse the determinist historians? Are we not replacing cultural or economic determinism with biological determinism? Not at all. First, to understand the principles governing the individual elements of a complex system is, as we have seen, not sufficient to be able to educe laws to predict the behavior of the whole ensemble. The beautiful paisleys of atmospheric turbulence are not explained by the most precise understanding of the individual properties—atomic weight, chemical structure, specific heat, and so on—of its elements. Second, the peculiar understanding of the human being that we are coming to is of a creature programmed rather rigidly and in certain specific ways to do something that is totally open-ended: to learn and to create. Our hard-wiring—whose proper development we neglect in our education at great peril—is designed to make us infinitely inventive. Our nature is a grammar which we must learn to use correctly, and which, if we do, makes us linguistically into protean gods, able to say anything in the world or out of it.

Thus the paradigm change which this line of argument suggests is from one in which a social universe of natureless, culturally determined units is governed by a set of causal laws and principles which, given precise input, will generate accurate predictions, to one in which a cultural universe of complex-natured but knowable individuals, by the interaction and feedback of their intentions, generates an ever-changing social pattern or paisley, which can be modelled but not predicted. The meaning of understanding would change from being able to give a discursive or mathematical account of something to being able to set up a working model that can do the same sorts of things as the original.

Fundamental political concepts like freedom, war, civil order, equality, literacy, power, justice, sovereignty, and so on would no longer be defined in terms of a set of objective abstract conditions but as living activities in a one-way unrepeatable process of historical change. It would be such a revaluation as occurred in literary criticism in the nineteenth century, when tragedy came to be defined as a process, an organic and recognizable activity, rather than as conforming to such rules as the Three Unities. Conceivably the automobile has done as much to create political freedom as any set of laws; yet historical and political scholarship is taken by surprise by such relationships. Perhaps one of the reasons why Eastern Europe became ungovernable by traditional socialist totalitarian means is that enough people had cars and telephones. Is not justice very much a matter of talent and personality? Blake said: one law for the ox and the lion is oppression. Might there not have been more equality of certain valid kinds between a gentleman and his valet than between an employer and employee in a classless society? Is not power the most questionable and fugitive of all concepts, seemingly so solid at one moment, but blown away by unpopularity the next? What is war in an age of terrorism, export dumping, military computer games, and nuclear standoff?

Such questions are not intended to induce the *aporia,* the bewilderment, of the mole-historian we depicted earlier, trying to define those troublesome ideas by the mere accumulation of data, so as to take into account all of the exceptions; rather, they are a preface to a new/old kind of historical understanding. Objective and abstract definitions of political concepts imply utopias, ideal principled social states towards which historical polities should strive; satisfy the definitions, and we have perfection, the end of history, an objective rationality to judge all of the past! Horrible idea; but it governs most political enthusiasm. Instead, let us imagine a peculiar kind of progress—not the old one, towards Whig empire or Hegelian state or proletarian or socialist or technological paradise, but a progress in changing terms which themselves progress by subsuming earlier ones; a progress that looks like decline or stagnation to those fixed to one idea of it; a progress not along a straight time-line but along one that curves back and fills up the holes in itself until it begins to look like a plane or a solid; a progress forged out of the evolutionary competition of totalizations, in which those most accommodating, most loving to each other, like the mammals, have the best chance of survival.

But is not progress an outdated concept? Even among the historians of science there are now those who deny any progress. Thomas Kuhn, the theorist of scientific revolutions, has publicly questioned whether there can be any improvement from one scientific paradigm to the next—say, from the Aristotelian to the Newtonian. Paul Feyerabend goes even further into scientific agnosticism. The deconstructionists all vehemently deny the possibility of progress. Likewise Robert Heilbroner and the Club of Rome. But all of these thinkers are caught in a logical trap, from which there is no escape. For either their own ideas are an improvement on those of their predecessors, in which case progress has occurred (and could in theory occur again), or they are no improvement, which implies there is no reason for us to take them seriously. In either case their ideas do not stand outside or above the process of history.

Since some notion of progress is thus a logical precondition of any attempt at understanding or argument, let us examine where the critics of progress go wrong. Kuhn argues that, because the criteria of coherence and explanation that Aristotle's science satisfied are different from the criteria met by Newton, to compare the two systems is to compare apples and oranges. The differences between the criteria themselves is a matter of values, not facts, and so no determination of superiority can be made between them. The assumption is that values are not real; and because this assumption is the key to an argument whose conclusion—there can be no progress—is manifestly self-contradictory, this assumption must be false. Values, then, are real. They are the "strange attractors" that emerge within the apparent chaos of historical events, relatively independent of the particular circumstances, and with their own beautiful structure. They are the fundamental motives of history and thus the indispensable criteria of scientific knowledge about human culture as such.

And here we may be in a position to begin to redeem that promise, of forms of understanding and descriptive categories proper to our own level of reflexive complexity, which we implied earlier. The real forces at work on the stage of history are *values*. And values are uniquely qualified for a role both as tools to understand history and as forces at work in it. One qualification is just that: they straddle the worlds of action and knowledge, they admit candidly our involvement, our partisanship, our partiality, and our power. Objectivity in an his-

torian is an impossible goal in any case. Another qualification
of values is that they give a kind of direction to history, the
possibility of progress, which as we have seen is the logical
precondition of any inquiry. Values are essentially dynamic,
readjusting, contested, and vigorous, as the word's derivation
from the Latin for "health," and its congnate "valor" imply.

We must reexamine those older partisan brands of historiography that wore their values on their sleeves: heroic, exemplary, mythic history. Perhaps their intellectual credentials were
not as shaky as we thought; perhaps they were not so naively
unaware of the possibility of their own bias. Herbert Butter-
field's critique of Herodotus is a lovely example of the way in
which the critic is ironically exposed by his material:

> He wrote history partly in order that great deeds (whether
> of Greeks or non-Greeks) should be placed on record, and
> partly because he wished to lay out the causes of the
> Greco-Persian war. He was interested in the way in which
> things came to happen and would look for rational explan-
> ations, showing the influence of climate and geographical
> factors and presenting excellent portrayals of character,
> though he was liable to impute important events to trivial
> incidental causes, the influence of women [sic] and purely
> personal factors. At the same time he had a disturbing
> sense of supernatural influences, showed the inadequacy
> of human calculations, the retribution that Heaven would
> inflict on great misdeeds, and introduced dreams, oracles,
> visions, and divine warnings of approaching evil. (Philip
> P. Wiener, ed., *Dictionary of the History of Ideas,* New
> York: Scribner's, 1973, 468.)

With Herodotus we might cite the great Roman historians,
Alfred and Shakespeare on English history, Vico, Burke, de
Tocqueville, Burkhardt, Huizinga, and Forrest Macdonald as
all in one way or another recognizing the fundamental importance of values as the driving force of history. Shakespeare
especially is an exemplary historian of the persuasion I wish
to urge; more than anyone else he sees how together we make
up the drama of history according to what we deem to be the
best, and how from that loom flows the rich pattern of human
events.

It might well be objected that I am advocating an outrageous
abandonment of objectivity, and giving license to the worst

forms of ethnocentrism and bias. Indeed I must plead guilty, but with mitigating circumstances. It was the age of "objective" history that provided the fuel for scientific racism, holocausts, colonialism, and the Gulag. The ideologue who believes he has objective truth on his side is more dangerous than the ordinary patriot or hero, because he calls his values "facts" and will disregard all ordinary human values in their service. We are going to be ethnocentric anyway; let us at least play our ethnocentrisms against each other on a level playing field and not attempt to get the objective high ground of each other. Given such a game, adaptive success in the long run attends those versions of our partisanship that have the widest, panhuman, appeal. Let us seek not to avoid bias, but to widen our bias in favor of the whole human race, and beyond.

This approach especially questions the apparent straightforwardness of the notion of political power. Events occur, and their meaning is rich and complex. The events are made up of the actions of men and women; and if they performed those actions then, tautologically, they had the power to do so. Do we gain anything by inserting the idea of power? Suppose they didn't perform the actions; could they have? Could we prove it? Power depends on values, and values on the individual and collective imagination.

Even the very methodology of historical research may have to be profoundly modified if the new view of history is to prevail. A perceptive critic of historiography, Gene Wise, has already pointed out some of the fallacies in the accepted model of historical research, in which "primary sources" (contemporary documents and suchlike) are valued more highly than secondary ones (such as later interpretations by historians), and they in turn are preferred over tertiary discussions and revisions of historical interpretations. He rightly declares that the only true primary source is the actual experience of the participants in historic events. All other sources are secondary and partial filters; but the nature of the filter itself is part of history, and perhaps a more crucial part than we think. R. G. Collingwood said: all history is the history of ideas. Or we might put it this way: history (small h) is History (capital H).

Perhaps we could go even further and remark that much contemporary documentation may paradoxically be worse evidence than later judgments by hindsight. Consider, as an analogy, the information-processing system of the human eye and visual cortex. If "primary" evidence is better than secondary, then the best visual data about what is happening in the "outside world" are the raw firings of the retinal neurons. The work of the optic nerve and visual cortex would amount to nothing more than a heap of opinion and sophistry. The military technologists who wanted to design an eye by which homing missiles might recognize their prey took this position at first, but they were soon proved wrong. Their attempt to hook up a TV camera to a simple computer programmed with pictures of enemy tanks simply did not work. The raw data did not add up to tanks but to a riot of shadows, colors, changes in reflectivity and albedo, geometric distortions by perspective, and confusing shifts which could not distinguish between subjective motion, motion of the object, changes in the object, and changes in light and shadow. To make a catalog of all the appearances a tank might take on would require a memory as big as the universe, which, moreover, could easily mistake something else for a tank. Later work by Artificial Intelligence researchers like Marvin Minsky and vision scientists like Edwin Land and David Marr revealed the astonishing hierarchy of ganged or independent servomechanisms that makes up vision, and its radical dependence on prior expectations, needs, actions, and questions to make any sense of the world at all. In other words, the secondary and tertiary sources are much more reliable than the primary ones, to use the old classification.

Further, of course, the physical world is, as quantum theory reminds us, constituted as such partly by the cooperation of sentient beings. Thus tanks don't look like tanks and can't act as tanks without being interpreted as tanks; their tank existence derives from the secondary and tertiary data. And of course this analogy is not simply an analogy, but also a further deconstruction even of Wise's notion of "experience." If the old hierarchy of primary and secondary is so problematic for visual experience itself, think what it is for the process of historical evidence-gathering. What history really is is our interpretation of it. We are all, in the deepest sense of experience, contemporary experiencers of those historical events; quite as much as the astronomers are contemporary experiencers of the supernova that exploded one hundred sixty million years ago and whose light has just now hit their telescopes. We can with relief relinquish the positivism of the old mainstream historical research; after all, the physicists abandoned it fifty years ago.

We can abandon, too, that kind of history which always assumes that there is a true, hidden version of events, of which the apparent surface is a hypocritical cover-up. Of course, hidden motives and interests do govern what goes on; but everybody has such motives, and everybody is a player in the game, a partner in the feedback. If the population is deceived, it may be because it wants to be deceived, and, if the deceiver is unveiled, will get itself a more competent magician and a more satisfying illusion. And such collective creations, in this contingent world of ours, verily constitute reality. The surface of history *is* the reality, and the new historiography will treat it as an expressive, meaningful, but inexhaustible artistic object, and seek not only to reveal an inner truth that derives from initial conditions or a conspiratorial *deus ex machina*.

This means that the capacity to recognize beauty, the esthetic sense, is the primary cognitive skill of the historian or sociologist. It is by beauty that we intuit the order of the reflexive process of human history. On the small, tribal scale the need for this essential function may well have been one of the principal selective pressures that led us toward our extraordinary inherited talents for storytelling and the interpretation of narrative. History should be refounded on story, not the other way around. Indeed, much of the most exciting new work in sociology—for instance the work of Thomas Scheff—is beginning to take this direction, and to break free from its positivistic traditions; cultural anthropology, with its participant-observer methods and its tradition of listening to native informants, did not have very far to go.

If the new definition of historical understanding is that we understand what we are able to model, and if our new definition of evidence is experience, how do we model and experience history?

I would suggest a number of ways, some of which are already being used unsystematically and without theoretical justification, but very effectively nonetheless. Almost all of them involve a greater or lesser degree of collapse between the activities of teaching, learning, and research—which would be no bad thing for our academies.

First, historical reenactments. Popular culture, as often, is ahead of the academy. The reenactment of Civil War battles and the battles of Texan independence has become a vital and creative popular movement. Historians should pay close attention; the experience of the "soldiers" is apparently extraordinarily intense and often not what one would expect. Of course, reenactment need not be confined to military events.

Second, ethnodrama, which is a new technique designed by

anthropologists and performance experts to enact central ritual or social activities from other cultures and periods—marriages, funerals, and other social dramas. The Smithsonian, to its credit, has recognized the historical value of this form of knowing by doing.

Third, the use of events taking place now, of which our experience is peculiarly sharp, to partially model past events. Those modern events may be the more useful as models because of their divergence from their analogue. For instance the current state of conflict in the Middle East may valuably model the Thirty Years' War in Germany and the other postrenaissance religious conflicts in Italy and France.

Fourth, war games and their extension into the diplomatic, social and economic spheres. War games have in the developed world now largely replaced actual battles as the most efficient way of resolving military struggle; even now we are still engaged in such a war with the Soviet Union, as we have been for some years. The actual weapons are little more than gold reserves, so to speak, kept in the bank to support the working currency, which is the games. Through our disarmament talks we are presently in the process of abandoning that "gold standard." With the advent of better computers we should be able to game-model a variety of historical situations and cultural processes, altering the parameters, variables, and degrees of feedback until we get a course of events which matches the historical data. The point is that the data need not be especially rich, or even reliable, to provide, as an ensemble, extremely rigorous and exclusive criteria to be satisfied by the model. Leontief's mathematical model of the economy of the United States is a nice example of what can already be done along these lines.

Finally I would suggest the careful attention to fictional and dramatic accounts of history, their performance, and even their fresh creation. This is a time-honored and enormously fruitful practice; but it may be even more fruitful if we treat it as serious historiography. Here we may test the validity of historical ideas by seeing whether the events of history are psychologically and narratively consistent with the fictional model.

We are perhaps now ready to apply Marx's dictum—that the point is not to understand history, but to change it—in a way quite different from what he intended. That art which changes history may be its most intimate and precise study.

10 Victor Turner and the Ghost of Hamlet's Father

My father, Victor Turner, the anthropologist and comparative religionist, was an exemplar of the kind of pedagogy which is implied by this book. Those who knew him and his work can testify to the extraordinary intellectual and creative energies he knew how to evoke in his teaching. It will be rewarding to examine how he did what he did.

Turner himself claimed during his life that any study of his methods was equivalent to a visit from the death angel. In the present case, as he would have said, the damage has already been done. We owe it to him to undertake this enterprise in his spirit—playfully, with eyes wide open, reflexively, alive to the ironic implications of all possible "meta" perspectives.

In fact, an examination of Turner's peculiar use of the "meta" mode is an excellent way to enter his work. Critics, whether they are performing arts theoreticians, historians, sociologists, philosophers, or of the literary persuasion, normally adopt the "meta" stance when they are engaged in covert ideological struggle, as when they are pushing a revisionist theory and want to avoid having to do battle on their enemy's ground. In other words, the "meta" perspective is used to distance, alienate, control, and delegitimate. Turner used the "meta" mode for an entirely different purpose. Without ulterior goals or ideological strategy, and without any implication that the revelation of rationale and intention devalued an action, he sought to confront the participants in an argument with their own and each other's inner motives. The purpose of his questioning would be fulfilled when the debaters met each other's eyes with a sheepish grin and that dawning affection which comes from the recognition of our common predicament as mortal self-conscious animals. He did this not in any spirit of hostility, manipulation, revision, or debunking, but in a spirit of comic frankness, insight, compassion, epiphany, and the acknowledgment of shared humanity. He always included himself in the revelation, and never used the "meta" as a way of getting the high ground of a person.

It may seem odd, then, that he would greet the prospect of such a thing as a methodological study, a "meta" genre in itself, upon which he was in turn taking an ironic "meta" perspective, with that only half-comic horror. But if we examine the metaphors he used to describe the origin, development, and establishment of enduring cultural structures, we will see why. For him cultural reality originated in the hot, liquid, protean fertility of *communitas,* in antistructure, in Dilthey's "experience," in charismatic liminality, "betwixt and between" the settled and solid states of social routine. This fecund seedbed would be sheltered from any charge of blasphemy by the plea that all action in this space was "only" subjunctive, only, so to speak, in quotation marks. Stylistically, Turner loved quotation marks and the subjunctive mood.

As time went by the participants in the original timeless moment of revelatory experience, or their followers, would seek to enshrine and preserve the original deposit of revelation, and thus its subjective concomitant of joy or insight, by crystallizing or encapsulating it in a husk of ritual, symbol, myth, and exegesis, a husk that would protect the seed or semantic content so that in another time it might blossom forth once more. Turner was fascinated by the way in which such a flowering might happen again and again in the great religions, and this partly accounts for his interest in pilgrimages, millenarian cults, and in figures like St. Francis. Culturally universal ways of preserving the deposit of spirit would tend to evolve: the concentric tripartite structure of life-crisis and calendrical ritual, for instance, with gated barriers—the rites of separation and reaggregation—guarding the sacred and irreverent liminal period within at its beginning and its end. This process carried with it, however, the risk of ossification, fossilization, and deadly routine. The live pores of the original spontaneous structure would be drained of their charismatic content, and the fiery liquid of joy and insight would be replaced by the embalming fluid of tradition, which would in turn harden into cold and rigid authority, until what was originally the cure for the petrifaction of human life would have become the chief symptom of the disease.

These were Turner's metaphors; what do they tell us about pedagogy? Obviously, that we must beware of taking structure and procedure as legitimate substitutes for spirit and charisma.

Our cultural holdings should be like seeds, tightly wound bundles of potential growth, rather than like ossified memorials to the inessentials of method and terminology. It was the process, not the structure, that contained the meaning.

It is important to distinguish Turner's position from that of the deconstructionists. Deconstructionist analysis, while professing to set us free from structural reduction and determinism, provides every text or cultural creation with exactly the same content: that all meanings are a dancing over the void, and that the void is fundamental. Turner believed that we all, civilized or "savage," know that already; and for him the dancing was so much more substantial than the void that our definition of reality might as well, since we are in linguistic control of it, be tailored to fit the dancing rather than the void. Then we would be ready to study the really interesting things, which are the dance and how to do it ourselves.

Where Turner agreed with the deconstructionists was in their rejection of the structuralist claim to exhaust the content of an object by exhausting its form. If a text is really a script for a ritual, pageant, or drama, we would not know the full content of it until it was performed, and then it might be very different the next time. But the contradictions in the script were not secret signs that the script was really meant to discredit itself; rather, they were meat for the actors, to make an effective show, full of conflict and suspense. And the actors must choose, and decide, and limit the meaning and content, and affirm it, if the show is to work. Deconstruction is not prepared to make this sacrifice, and therefore cannot perform.

Turner's own teaching was in itself an example of how the spirit, locked in its textual husk, might be set free. His seminars were like rituals of invocation, of resurrection. No method, no structure, adequately explains what he did. What then? Should the enterprise of applying Turner's ideas to the practice of pedagogy be abandoned? Should we at least avoid giving them careful and systematic consideration, and concentrate instead on an impressionistic attempt to reproduce his spirit? Paradoxically, Turner was an exceedingly careful, scholarly, exact, and scientific thinker himself, and to be in his spirit is to follow him as much in this as in his emotional tone. The only way of resolving this paradox is by positing a whole new conception of the academy itself, one pioneered in Turner's own pedagogy and already taking root here and there among the universities. It is only in the light of this notion of the academy, and this conception of the proper ends and energies of pedagogy, that a genuine postmodernism can evolve.

Characteristically, Turner seldom made an issue of his inter-disciplinary approach in itself, and never promulgated it as an ideology or a crusade. Instead, he quietly and radically got on with his work, without advertising its implications, fatal though they were to established notions of academic study. When he found the disciplinary restrictions of an institution too confining, he either changed the nature of his relationship with it or simply pulled up stakes and left. But a set of assumptions can be inferred from his practice, and they have a crucial bearing on pedagogy.

The traditional model of the subject matter of academic research can be visualized, as I suggested in chapter 8, as a flat plane extending in all directions, divided by natural boundaries into "fields of study." The annual intake of students is judiciously distributed over this expanse and individually encouraged to choose a particular field, on the basis of inclination, need, and receptivity to training. It is expected that a student will give some attention to those fields which immediately adjoin his or her own, though this interest should not be too great and should be comically self-deprecatory in tone, as a ritual appeasement gesture to the territorial occupiers. In addition, a personally broadening hobby may be chosen, preferably in a field utterly unconnected with the student's specialty. Thus a sort of landscape appears, like one conceived by ants or termites, individually blind to the big picture, but collectively capable of remarkable feats of architecture. Over the plain hover wise and benign administrators, showering financial resources, adjudicating territorial disputes, and reporting the results to society at large. Each field possesses its own characteristic jargon, whose secret passwords and signs are jealously guarded by the high priests, and revealed to initiates only after humiliating and protracted ordeals. At the edges of the worked area, heroic groundbreaking scholars hack out new fields from the wilderness, while empire-building department heads seize and temporarily hold neighboring territories. When the work of one field becomes too difficult for the average trained researcher, the field splits into subfields, which may slowly attain the status of fields in themselves.

Over this landscape Turner wandered like some prophet of apocalypse. To the inhabitants of a given field he could demonstrate all of the qualifications required of an expert; but then he could be seen, disquietingly, several fields away, conversing with the elders of the temple in their own language; and then again, was hailed in yet another place as a systematizer or a groundbreaker. Worse than this, he acted as if the divisions between the fields were not essential or indigenous in themselves, and laid bare the uncomfortable implications of the fact that if accepted fields were once subfields, then either their present boundaries are arbitrary or we would have no assurance that undiscovered rifts might lie below our feet, waiting to swallow us up in destruction like the San Andreas fault. Worse still, he showed again and again that the answer to a problem in one field usually lay in plain view in another; he sometimes acted as if one field actually interpenetrated another or even lay superimposed upon it, so that, as it were, one could be in two places at once. A master of jargon, he was often entrusted by the high priests with the most sacred words in their discipline; but then he would turn around and betray their trust by showing that the best and most paradigmatic definition of those words was in the terms of another discipline altogether. (For instance, consider his dramatistic redefinition of social redress procedures, or his political analysis of the ritual of Becket's martyrdom, or his New Critical treatment of Ndembu ritual symbols, or his resocialization of Freud, or his Blakean/Hegelian/Marxist explanation of traditional rites and ceremonies.) When the territory of a given discipline was human, he refused to acknowledge the distinction between researcher and object of study, and recruited gifted native informants as collaborators, guides, or even research directors (as in his essay on Muchona the Hornet). One of the essential properties of the old model was that the researcher is more conscious and aware than the object of research; Turner often assumed precisely the opposite.

But it is important to distinguish Turner's approach from what is usually considered to be "interdisciplinary." Oddly enough, the interdisciplinary does have a place in the old model, as a sort of permitted travel, tourism, or diplomacy, with much obeisance to the mutual untranslatability of disciplinary languages, and courtly deference to foreign customs. Interdisciplinary studies are marked as anomalous but as an allowed luxury or even perversion reserved for the expert. Nobel prizewinners are given visas to travel in other fields, but their visits are state visits. Interdisciplinary study by younger researchers can sometimes be the first symptoms of fission or of parturition in the field, and is often approved because the resulting new discipline is even smaller, more jealous of its boundaries, and more supportive of the general disciplinary ideology, than an older and more easygoing field. Of course, one can always rise above the disciplinary boundaries by becoming an administrator; but then one is expected to give up any creative work—as it is defined in the model. Turner was in fact often nudged in this direction but resisted it to the end.

In the old model the truth is like an unknown landscape, fully formed and uncontradictory in itself, which when explored is known at first in a fragmentary and apparently contradictory way, but which eventually yields up its secrets and submits to an exact accounting, the contradictions having been ironed out. Turner was content to accept this model for the physical sciences, though indeed his skepticism about its general application might well be confirmed by the extraordinary logic of quantum mechanics; he certainly denied it as appropriate to the study of human beings as persons in society. For him human truth was the characteristic vitality of the growing edge of a system, its living cambium, and the mind of the thinker about human truth was part of that growth, and vital to it. The growth process—and here he never forgot what he had learned from Marx—was inherently contradictory, and the resolution of its paradoxes was the clearest sign of its death. "Without Contraries is no Progression," from Blake, was one of his favorite quotations, as was Whitman's "Do I contradict myself? Very well, I contradict myself."

This is not to say that he did not seek consistency and logical coherence; indeed he was quite a formidable reasoner. Rather, he knew that if an idea was strong and vital enough, it would generate a new paradox for every one that it resolved; like Niels Bohr, he felt that the opposite of a profound truth is another profound truth. Our appetite for consistency was the very drive that revealed the richest paradoxes. What he resisted was the tendency to reject an idea or fact the moment it generated a contradiction. Another of his sayings was "beware of premature closure."

Implicit in Turner's practice was a different conception of the academic life. Although he was deeply suspicious of morality, he was actually engaged in a profoundly moral enterprise, the life devoted to what he called "ideas" and to personal love—and he did not clearly distinguish between the two. He loved the free, idiosyncratic, creative intelligence in other people, and though he was interested in their other characteristics he was not especially fond of them. For him it was no longer enough to be expert in a field—though he demanded expertness as a necessary but not sufficient requirement for serious thinking. It was not enough to keep abreast of developments in a field, or even in several fields, if this was done without judgment, question, or imaginative intervention. To be a real thinker one needed actively to explore many fields, with a developing core of ideas in search of confirmation or deconfirmation. One had to be prepared to learn new languages or modes of discourse at any stage in one's life. And the great tool for this research, this exploration, and new learning, was teaching. Turner's seminars always ventured out into new material, the teacher and the students in the same boat, the students learning by his example how to learn, how to make mistakes, and correct them, and find out why the mistake was made, and achieve original new insight in the field as a result. The classroom was the laboratory.

Turner simply did not recognize the disciplinary boundaries. His mode of the interdisciplinary took all human life as its subject, and assumed a total organic relationship between all of its aspects, so that information obtained in one disciplinary mode simply could not be understood at all except in the context of all the others. If Turner's approach were to be translated into institutional organization, it would require the universities to abolish departments altogether. If his assumptions about education, and those of his collaborators and successors, take root, the change in the academy will be a massive alteration in the structure of legitimation, in the conception of what constitutes a subject, in the definitions of information, proof, and investigation, in the accreditation of academic personnel.

Hence the legacy Victory Turner left to the academy includes, for instance, the notion that there is no legitimate "literary" criticism as such; literature is part of a spectrum of ritual and "rituoid" human activities (to coin a term), and its investigation may take us at once into neuroanatomy and psychophysics, economics, theology, kinship studies, political philosophy, theater, and our own personal lives. Literature is no more one of the humanities than it is one of the social sciences, the arts, or the life sciences.

So our original enterprise, which was to examine Turner's contribution to pedagogy, has led us to a larger critique of the structure of the academy itself. But if we abandon the traditional departmental boundaries and the model of study which they imply, what will replace them? If we could be assured of a reliable supply of authentic geniuses with a charismatic gift of communication, we could simply sit them down under the trees with some students and leave them to it. Failing this, we need some kind of structure. In his later years Turner developed a remarkable method of teaching, which combined his profound knowledge of the dynamics of human rituals of celebration, initiation, and invocation, sophisticated theatrical and performance techniques, a developing theory of human motivation and brain reward, and classical ideas of debate, dialectic, and symposium. His pedagogy took three main forms: the seminar, the ethnodrama, and the dithyrambic speech.

"Turner's midnight seminar," as it was called by his students, was always held at his home, and his wife and collaborator Edie was always involved. It began around 7:45 in the evening, when the first students began to arrive. They would drink coffee—for at this point a keyed up, high concentration, close attention mode was called for. Groups of people would gather in the porch, the kitchen, the living room, the garden. It was an explicit part of the ritual that the normal boundaries between the academic and the domestic were broken down; this was no exclusive symposium of males, in refuge from Xanthippe, but a full heir of that mixed company which gathered in the castle at Urbino to hear discourses of love, virtue, and courtiership and be recorded by Castiglione. About 8:15 everyone would be rounded up to hear the paper that was being read that evening. About five minutes into the paper the first interruption would come; a question, objection, or elaboration by one of the reader's fellow students. Often the interruption would lead to debate and discussion, given full rein because everyone knew that there would be all the time the world to talk everything out, and nobody need go home with ideas pent up inside. At last the discussion would circle back to the paper, and so it would go on, in a helical fashion, adding an increment each time the talk returned to the paper. There is something comfortable about the digressive mode; it sweeps up all loose ends in its passing.

After a while the audience and the reader would be fully "in sync," a state signalled by the fact that interruptions would elicit from the reader the plea that "I'm coming to that." The talk would rise to a climax, everyone talking at once, often summed up by Turner himself, with a general feeling of high excitement, of insight, connection, epiphany. Then there would be a beer break, with pretzels and crunchy snacks, because people would be feeling oral, aggressive, wanting to get their teeth into something. The beer was a mild brain reward for the hard mental work that was being done; the seminar was using the genre of the party or celebration—to teach by delighting. Arguments between pairs, trios, or quartets of people would now arise, merge, break into subdisputes, or go to someone else for corroboration, expert advice, or judgment. The mood became more relaxed as the group reconvened to share the results of the individual discussions. Around 11:30 some people would begin to leave but a hard core of four or five would stay on to around one o'clock, talking by the front door, unwilling to leave, and sometimes end up in an all-night bar to continue the conversation.

A major feature of the seminar was the moment when Turner himself would get "fired up" and begin to develop a point raised in the paper or discussion. An extraordinary eloquence possessed him at those times, an exactness of memory for fact and quotation, combined with a candor and directness of manner, an engaging humor, and a willingness to venture into poetic and mystical language—though he never lost the fierce probity of his scientific skepticism. This speech was not so much lecture as the voicing of a collective intelligence that had formed itself during the course of the evening; there was even something of the shaman, the Dionysian priest, or sacrificial victim in the feel of it, something both solemn and hilarious. Personal affection and even love were implicit in the generosity of the speech and in the attention of the hearers. In this state of mind insight was possible that would be inaccessible in a more conventional, "cooler" academic mood. To put this more strongly, scholarly detachment in the western tradition, though valuable for many uses, can actually prevent intellectural discovery.

A major element of Turner's pedagogy was the ethnodrama. In order to understand—and make his students understand—what was going on in another culture, Turner took the most direct route, which was through firsthand experience of it. In his fieldwork Turner entered into close personal friendships with the people he studied, and went through exactly the same hermeneutic spiral of mutual attunement of signification that a child does when it achieves the culturally impossible and, starting from utter strangerhood, becomes a full-fledged member of the community: "Except ye become as a little child." Turner put his students through the same experience, by assigning them roles in the alien community, and making them act through some major life-crisis, together with its central ritual. His directorial instructions included the rules, taboos, kinship conventions, and actual historical background of the event; and the students had to prepare the ritual garments, decorations, sacred objects, music, food, and gifts required for the occasion. These preparations could take days or weeks, and after a while it simply became easier for the students to stay in their roles, once they got used to them, than to be continuously translating back and forth from the ethnographic, detached mode.

Staying in character was nevertheless difficult at times, just as it is in real life; I don't have a script to tell me what is in character for me, and must make it up as I go along, helped by my fellow actors on this great stage of fools. The fact that a given brain can support dozens of different authentic selves is well known from studies of split personality; sanity consists perhaps in the cooperative choice of one of them, a choice which—to use the language of theater—bears profound resemblances to the actor's choice of objective. Turner's ethnodramas, then, had all the genuine *in*authenticity and artificiality of actual human life; except that the commitment to the fiction may have been greater than in the original, because the participants, coming to it fresh and with the enthusiasm of an absorbing game, might have been enjoying it more.

Another way of expressing the beautiful and profound paradoxes implicit in Turner's ethnodrama is that, for him, the natural organ of human social interaction was the imagination, and the only way of truly experiencing something at *first* hand is through the imagination. Thus anyone who tells us that they have had an experience that we cannot imagine for ourselves, but must go through it, is talking nonsense; for to imagine it is to go through it—is the only way of going through it. Our greatest contemporary problem may not be the limited experience modern people have of other people's conditions of life, but the fact that they are not taught to imagine, and therefore to feel, even their own experience. All the world's a stage.

Turner's pedagogical practice is confirmed by new advances in the theory of language teaching. The old analytical method, whereby the student learns the grammar and vocabulary before attempting to use the language, and the more recent "language-lab" system, which attempts by a sort of mechanized operant conditioning to program the language into the student, have been shown to contain equal, though different, weaknesses and flaws. The new method is by a high-intensity, high-affect dramatic environment, in which teacher and students generate *ad hoc* dramatic situations and are forced by the exigencies of conflict and desire to invent effective language on the spot, as the child must, growing up in a family. This technique is really a rediscovery, and it has proved remarkably successful.

Turner staged African and Dixieland weddings, pilgrimages, curing rituals, even funerals. The last funeral in which he participated was his own, a full-scale Ndembu funeral for a chief, with drum music, masked dancers, a seclusion hut for the widow, communal dancing, much drinking, tears, laughter, and reminiscence. It was put on at Turner's house by his friends, family, students and colleagues in anthropology, religious studies, and the performing arts, using Turner's own meticulous field notes on the proper conduct of the ritual. All concerned were deeply moved—many of the participants dreamed about Turner shortly afterwards, and many have felt his presence in their lives since as a creative and energizing influence. The absurdity of this strange event, the curious element of comedy that we all felt in it, was entirely in the spirit of the Ndembu ritual itself, which partly consists of the personification of the deceased's death as a grotesque and absurd figure, and a comic mocking of it until is subdued and made familiar. The person who played the role of Turner's death, in a gorgeous and terrifying feathered mask of red, white, and black, a distinguished professor of anthropology, counts it as one of the central experiences in his life. (The strap for the costume, which was not well adjusted, cut a wound in his skin which he did not feel until the next day.)

Skeptics might well object that this ritual was inauthentic because it was done consciously and reflexively, in a meta-mode, so to speak. But Turner's research had showed that all live human rituals are already "meta"; reflexivity is not just a feature of the sophisticated postmodernist work of art—the novel, say, that introduces its author as a character—but is the normal condition, even part of the function, of the major human rituals. This may have been one of Turner's greatest insights: there never were any innocent unconscious savages, living in a state of unreflective and instinctive harmony. We human beings are all and always sophisticated, conscious, capable of laughter at our own institutions, inventing our lives collectively as we go on, playing games, performing our own being. This is our specialization as animals, our nature. The true naîveté is the naîveté of modern or postmodern intellectuals who believe that they are the inventors of social criticism, existential insecurity, and metaperspectives. The mainstream culture that they attack is actually more self-aware than they are, because its rituals of reflexiveness are older and more finely tuned than theirs. We simply have to relearn how to do them properly.

For precisely this reason, Turner was fascinated by classical and folk genres in literature: epic, liturgy, drama, tales, and jokes. He preferred poetry in traditional meters—the hymn-tunes of Blake, the sonnets of Rilke and Hopkins, the tight metrical structures of the French symbolists, the terza rima of Dante, the pentameter of Shakespeare—perhaps because meter is an ancient psychic technology to achieve that quasi-trance state of heightened awareness which he had found in ritual. He loved narrative, plot, character, drama—those elements often abandoned by modernist experimenters as embodying what they took to be the complacency of established society, and ignored by modernist critics as sugarcoating on the pill; he saw in them instead the keys to cultural self-examination, self-criticism, and self-transcendence. For him exegesis was part of the ritual, criticism part of the performance of literature, analysis a practical tool in the invention and construction of cultural reality.*

*We often take Western Culture as if it were a single, monolithic organization ruled by such sinister abstractions as Rationality, Patriarchy, Commodity Fetishism, and Hierarchy, ignoring the evident contradictions between these ideas. In doing so we commit the very intellectual sin that the West is usually convicted of without trial: the reduction of human individuals and community to a generalized Other, as in the celebrated early anthropological solecism "The African likes his meat rotten." I can remember clearly at a conference a Western academic critic of Western attitudes, eager to deconstruct the hegemonic rationality of the West, verbally embracing a Hindu scholar with praise for Indian nonrationality and nondualism, and the icy embarrassment of the latter as he explained that in the 4,000 years of Indian philosophy every form of rationality and dualism had been espoused at various times. Of course monism and irrationalism have received beautifully clear articulations in Western philosophy and

The best way of demonstrating Turner's legacy is perhaps
in practice. Of course even the idea of what constitutes "practice" changes with the advent of a new paradigm. Practice for
the New Critics meant the formal analysis of a text—implicitly,
by an individual in the study, free of historical or biographical
constraints. Practice for Turner meant a group's ability to
perform a cultural script, with the same unpredictable richness
of new content as in the original performance. Turner's method
did not exclude analysis; but analysis was only one of the
means, a rehearsal and directorial technique, not the object of
the exercise. Nonetheless it might be interesting to judge the
results of putting Turner's method to work on a classical crux
in dramatic literature.

The classical crux I have chosen is in Shakespeare's *Hamlet*.
It is the question of the nature of Hamlet's change after he
returns from his aborted trip to England. Many critics are
implicitly—and sometimes explicitly—disappointed by Hamlet's
transformation from the brooding meditative critic of society
into the mere man of action, and miss his marvelous soliloquies
(which he gives up in act 5). Why should the Ghost's command
be such a problem for him at first, and then be so casually
accepted and acted upon at the end? Has Hamlet lost his moral
sensitivity? Is Shakespeare really a sort of inspired hack, filling
out an orthodox revenge tragedy with wonderful custom-made
philosophy, which is forgotten when the time comes for the
bloody payoff at the end? Or, to put it in Freudian terms,
what, at the end, has happened to Hamlet's interesting Oedipus
complex? It doesn't seem to bother him any more, but this is
not because he has talked it out with an analyst and thus got
it out of his system; the issue simply seems to go away. He
doesn't even mention his father in act 5 except for a very
detached and offhand reference to him as his former sovereign.
Has Hamlet, or worse still, Shakespeare, just swept the matter

Western folk practice. One of the greatest of all cultural gulfs yawns
between the Brahmins of our own academic/artistic caste and the
many cultures of contemporary Western civilization. We artists and
intellectuals are alienated also from our own cultural past, and need to
learn how to bring the same delicate concern for cultural integrity
and individuality to past phases of our own heritage that we have
learned to bring to the geographical and political Other. When we
take as our Third World our own cultural ancestors, the leap of
creative insight must join cultures that are separated not by space but
by time.

under the carpet? Part of the problem may be that critics, who are specialists, simply cannot imagine somebody being able to philosophize *and* to fight—let alone to take political action. But this is an explanation of the critic, not of the text.

Some years ago my "Shakespeare in Performance" seminar took on this issue, though it arose not in the form of a critical crux, as I have described it here, but in action. An account of this encounter may clarify some of the strengths of Turner's approach.

The context, significantly enough, is important. My seminar group was made up of American English majors from Kenyon College who were spending a year at the University of Exeter in England; I was *in loco parentis* for the group, and there was a more than usually close relationship among us all. Although I have often held seminars at home, this one took place in an ordinary classroom on campus; it was important to domesticate the academy in this case, and we took trouble to make the room our own by rearranging it, by bringing food and drink, and by marking our activity there with a curious combination of comic levity and sacred seriousness.

I had explained to the group my own ideas of the relationship between performance and the performative mode in philosophy, wherein a statement can be a speech act and bring its meaning truly into being by its utterance; and I had made the connection between drama and ritual, with reference to medieval religious theater, extending the concept to include the classroom itself. The classroom, I claimed, could support an alternate reality, as could any gathering where "two or three are gathered together" in a performative community. I had also related recent research in the brain chemistry of communal ritual trance to renaissance theories of memory, creativity, theater, art, and reality, referring to Frances Yates's work on the memory theater and to Shakespeare's own words about the poet's pen in *A Midsummer Night's Dream*. (At the end of the term we were to stage the last act of *The Winter's Tale,* in which a queen is apparently brought back from the dead, as the genuine invocation of a spirit—Shakespeare's own; but this is another story.)

The class method was as follows. Each student was assigned to direct a scene from Shakespeare, casting it from the class, and recording the rehearsal process for an essay that would be due later. The rest of the class voted on the performance, and the actors, the director, and any other stage personnel would all get the same grade. In other words, the performing group stood or fell together, and the reward system demanded that it please, move, and inspire a real, experienced, and perceptive audience. As the year went on the productions became more and more elaborate, daring, polished (and time-consuming in rehearsal). The students were addicted, and some performed many times more than I had required. They began to use costume, scenery, makeup, even lights and special effects, improvising with great ingenuity in our drab little classroom, and decorating it festively when appropriate. The grading system was soon forgotten, and we had to remind ourselves to keep it going. Some students even protested their own grades when they thought them too high! There was an electric sense of artistic enterprise and integrity.

After each show there was a long discussion, going late into the evening in the Turnerian fashion, and interrupted by food and coffee breaks. The discussion began on the most practical level, about blocking, staging, movement, props, and so on; but at each point the choices made by the directors and the actors pointed to more and more fundamental issues of interpretation and artistic purpose. We would go back to the text, then return to the performance, with each swing around the hermeneutic spiral yielding new insight. The actors' and directors' accounts of discoveries made in rehearsal, the little breakthroughs of pace and emphasis, carried us naturally to the personal experience of the participants upon which they drew for their interpretation of the parts, and thus to a close discussion of the psychological and moral depths of the play. Various strategies—modern dress, expressionist acting technique, operatic style; even, memorably, one hilarious evening, outrageous drag—were tried out and criticized. The criticism, though honest, was always gentle and generous; after all, the actor you were criticizing this week might be playing opposite you the next, or directing you, or even judging your performance. The emphasis, though, was always on the work as art; there was none of that philistine professionalism that one sometimes encounters in practical drama classes, where the sense of theater as another world is lost, and it has all become just work and procedure like any other job, with a nice smile for the rubes who pay to get in. Our seminar was an end in itself, a sacred and comic space whose rules were those of beauty and ritual validity.

One of our principles was that there were always an infinite

number of ways that one could play a scene, but that one could
only play one of them at a time, and some were more moving,
profound, funny, or enlightening than others. In deciding on
the theoretical underpinnings of our performance practice, we
rejected alike the doctrines of objective correctness, relativism,
pluralism, and subjectivism. Objective correctness was clearly
impossible; relativism, because it makes no choices, bored the
audience; pluralism wouldn't play; and subjectivism did not
last very long in an environment where everyone had to
cooperate to make the show work. What we had to aim for was
an evolving intersubjective attunement, which would pay for
itself by some act, comic or sacrificial, carrying the community
into personal insight.

Some time into the year, when we were all comfortable, we
took on act 5, scene 1 of *Hamlet,* the graveyard scene. The
performance began with a reading by the lead actor of a telegram from America, saying that his father had just died of a
coronary thrombosis, and that arrangements were being made
to fly the actor over for the funeral the following day. The
audience did not know whether this information was genuine
or not; it is a testimony to the nature of our group that it was
plausible that a student actor might, under such circumstances,
choose to share such news with the rest of us, and elect to go
on with the show. (To our relief, the telegram was not genuine;
but the actor had, as it were, trusted the sacred "good luck" of
the group enough to feel that his pretence would not tempt
fate. The students knew the story of Edward Alleyn, the Elizabethan actor who had played Doctor Faustus half a mile away
and four hundred years ago in Exeter; how in the damnation
scene it was noticed that there was one devil too many, and
how Alleyn had worn a crucifix under his shirt thereafter
whenever he played that part again.)

The room then went into total darkness. A candle was lit,
revealing Charles, the lead actor, putting on his makeup in a
mirror. He did it very slowly and carefully, with a look of extraordinary but restrained grief on his face. Then the stage was
set. Alison, who played the gravedigger, was normally a pain-
fully shy young woman; her voice broke when she read a paper
aloud. On stage, however, she was utterly transformed; she
could muster a queenly dignity or a commanding comic
authority, and was quite capable of a beautiful and outrageous
Rosalind, or a devious and innocent Cleopatra. She moved
among the audience and selected four of them, with whose

bodies she constructed a grave in the middle of the room. She did this with a natural and kindly grace which had behind it a rather steely insistence. The director was not afraid of the absurdity of this piece of business; after all, Peter Quince and Bottom had brought in a human wall to their play, and had been rewarded by a vision of the fairy powers of creation and a royal command to perform.

The scenes of gallows humor followed in a manic mood of grotesque comedy; the skulls were cabbages. At the moment that Hamlet reveals himself, Charles, who is a gentle and quiet person, blazed with frightening strength and maturity: "This is I, Hamlet the Dane," he said, and descended into the human grave, the "living monument" of Ophelia. At that moment something odd happened. The scene came to a climax of very intense feeling, the audience got the idea that the scene was over—directors were allowed to cut as much as they liked—and somebody miscued and turned the lights out. There was to be an ending to the scene and then a postscript in which Charles would first divest himself of Hamlet and then of the actor role he had assumed. The players decided to cut at that point and quit while they were ahead; and the audience's applause was interrupted by anxious inquiries about Charles's father. We all had the sense that some important ritual had been achieved.

In discussion layer after layer of exegesis was revealed. The group as a whole was feeling its strangerhood in England and missing home and America, and Charles's "telegram" expressed the secret fears of many. Hamlet has been summoned back from college at Wittenberg—Faust's university—for his father's funeral, and more recently has just returned from a journey whose original destination was England, and whose original purpose was the betrayal and death of Hamlet. The "common theme" was "death of fathers." The previous year I had been told, in the middle of a seminar on Dante, of my own father's heart attack; and the methods we were using to understand Shakespeare were partly fathered by him. Shakespeare's anxiety about his own various fathers, literal and metaphorical, is obvious in the play. John Shakespeare was probably drinking himself to death when the play was written, and he died not long after. (John Aubrey's anecdote gives drink as the cause of William Shakespeare's death as well.) The resemblance of Hamlet's name to that of Shakespeare's own recently dead son Hamnet could not have been lost on him. More than this,

Shakespeare was competing with various dramatic fathers: the mythical Greek dramatists, as yet unavailable to the Elizabethans; the stoic Roman tragedian Seneca, mentioned in the players' advertisement in 2.2. (and whose plays were being staged by "the little eyases," the rival boys' companies); and Shakespeare's predecessors in the revenge tragedy genre, including perhaps the author of a lost earlier version of *Hamlet*. Hamlet himself feels the pressure on him of the great classical heroes and gods, who were never at a loss for suitable heroic action—Hyperion, Mars, Mercury, Orestes, Pyrrhus, Hector, Ajax, Caesar; and of course Hercules and Alexander, both mentioned in 5.1. These are the fathers in the face of whom he must find or forge an identity. Eliot's Prufrock, like Stoppard's Rosencrantz and Guildenstern, thinks that Hamlet finds it easy to be a hero: "No, I am not Prince Hamlet, nor was meant to be;" but it is no easier for him to deal with his giants than for them to deal with theirs.

Perhaps the chief obstacle faced by the student actors was the invisible presence of the great British Shakespearean actors that they had seen on tape and would see—in the 1984 Stratford *Hamlet*—in the flesh a few days later. How to avoid cliché? This was the same question as, How to obey the father while being true to the father's own spirit of heroic independence? These questions were not lost on me, either, in my own state of recent bereavement, and the students knew it; one of them had also been in that seminar when I was called to deal with my father's fatal illness. But there was more yet: here in England, especially, I was their substitute father, and I had laid upon them this assignment to act the achievement of the prince. My own pedagogy is explicitly one of the handing over of power to my young successors, as Sarastro does in *The Magic Flute*—an enfranchisement which is also a challenge. Charles and Alison and the director, Steve, were tossing back the challenge with this radical and unorthodox interpretation of a play on which I had written a long chapter of a book eighteen years before.

So what was happening when Charles jumped into the grave, claiming a name and title which in combination could only belong to Hamlet's father? We were coming close to the significance of the catharsis we had felt, and we felt it again as the discussion proceeded: approach to the meaning restores the experience, said T. S. Eliot. Why doesn't Hamlet still have the same feeling of resistance against obeying his father (his Roman and Greek predecessors, the clichéd conventions of revenge tragedy, even his creator Shakespeare)? Because he has *become* them. He is their grave, where they are buried. This is I, Hamlet the Dane. Hamlet defeats the treacherous mission of Rosencrantz and Guildenstern by sealing his own substitute message with his father's seal ring, taking upon himself his father's literary person: a forged identity in both senses. By becoming the grave in which our fathers are buried, we eat them up and continue their life in our own bodies. When Charles jumped into the grave the student became the teacher, the stranger the native, the American the Englishman, the son the father, the anti-play the paradigmatic revenge tragedy, the modern intellectual the ancient Greek or Roman hero, the satyr Hyperion. Hamlet had been "too much i' th' son;" now he has become the sun king. At last he is able to make his public declaration of love for the woman he would have made his queen: "I loved Ophelia..."—his leap is not back into his mother's womb but into his wife's grave, and they are not the same. "Let Hercules himself do what he may,/ The cat will mew, and dog will have his day." Paradoxically, he is enabled to take on an independent identity by accepting his father's as his own.

The price of this change is an intimacy with death, a solidarity with it; we must become our fathers' death, even affirm it, and in so doing affirm our own. The secret reason why we fear to take up the position our fathers have left us is that we fear to die ourselves; until our father dies, we are immortal, for he stands between us and death, and shelters us from it with his brave old body. If we take up his identity, then we will die ourselves. To choose to succeed is to choose to die. To inherit is to join the party of the moribund. Death taxes are a magic to ward off death, so that we can hide from death when he comes for us, by claiming that we are not our father.

But how do we choose to become "Hamlet the Dane"? When Charles put on his makeup—actually he was miming it—he was taking upon himself his sacred face, his real soul. We become what we are by acting it up to the hilt; we don't discover what we are by introspection or analysis. The mirror and the candle were not instruments of investigation so much as instruments of creation. Our true selves are our played selves; and should anyone engage in a little trial of realities, theirs against ours, and we are prepared, as Hamlet is, to stake our lives upon the identity we have taken on, our critics can scarcely "impone," as Osric puts it, a bigger wager. Let us see which of us survives—the one who is too sophisticated to choose an identity, the pluralist, the relativist—or the one who has, by putting on the costume of the actor, promised his body to the grave. This madness might turn out to be sanity in the end.

To claim Victor Turner's legacy may, then, be a liberation more frightening than we bargained for. We may be called upon to deal with the contemporary artistic and intellectual scene as Hamlet deals with Denmark, that prison where something is rotten, and the times are out of joint and must be set right. We may have to venture into realms of deep embarrassment, of laughter at what we do not wish to laugh at, and of seriousness or sacredness that we do not associate with avant-garde cool. We may have to act a part for which we feel unready. But as the two funerals I have described seem to show, we might find our true identity in the process.

FURTHER READING

Alexander Argyros, "Prescriptive Deconstruction," *Critical Texts,* forthcoming.

Mikhail Bakhtin, *The Dialogic Imagination,* trans. Michael Holquist (Austin: University of Texas Press, 1981).—*Rabelais and His World,* trans. Helene Iswolsky (Cambridge: M.I.T. Press, 1968).

Stewart Brand, *The Media Lab: Inventing the Future at M.I.T.* (New York: Viking, 1987).

Fernand Braudel, *The Mediterranean and the Mediterranean World in the Age of Philip II* (3 vols.), trans. Sian Reynolds (New York: Harper & Row, 1972).

Edward Bruner and Victor W. Turner, eds., *The Anthropology of Experience* (Urbana: University of Illinois Press, 1986).

Joseph Campbell, *The Hero With a Thousand Faces* (Princeton: Princeton University Press, 1949).

R. G. Collingwood, *The Idea of History* (Oxford: Oxford University Press, 1946).

Robert P. Crease and Charles C. Mann, *The Second Creation: Makers of the Revolution in 20th-Century Physics* (New York: Macmillan, 1986).

E. G. D'Aquili, C. D. Laughlin, Jr., and J. McManus, eds., *The Spectrum of Ritual: A Biogenetic Structural Analysis* (New York: Columbia U.P., 1979).

Paul Davies, *God and the New Physics* (New York: Touchstone, 1983). —*The Cosmic Blueprint* (New York: Simon & Schuster, 1988).

Sir John Eccles, Roger Sperry, Ilya Prigogine, Brian Josephson, *Nobel Prize Conversations* (Dallas, San Francisco, New York: Saybrook, 1985).

John Miles Foley, ed., *Oral Tradition* (Columbia, Missouri) (periodical).

J. T. Fraser, "Out of Plato's Cave: The Natural History of Time," *Kenyon Review,* Winter, 1980. —*Time as Conflict* (Basel, Stuttgard: Birkhauser, 1978)

William Gibson, *Neuromancer* (New York: Ace, 1986).
— *Count Zero* (New York: Ace, 1987).

James Gleick, *Chaos: Making a New Science* (New York: Viking, 1987).

Erving Goffman, *The Presentation of Self in Everyday Life* (New York: Anchor, 1959).
— *Interaction Ritual* (New York: Anchor, 1967).

David Griffin, ed., *The Reenchantment of Science* (Albany: SUNY Press, 1988).
— *God and Religion in the Postmodern World* (Albany: SUNY Press, 1989).

James Hans, *The Play of the World* (Amherst: University of Massachusetts Press, 1981).

Charles Hartshorne, *Born to Sing: an Interpretation and World Survey of Bird Song* (Bloomington: Indiana University Press, 1973).

Ihab Hassan, "The Question of Postmodernism," in Harry R. Garvey, ed., *Romanticism, Modernism, Postmodernism* (Lewisburg, Toronto, and London: Bucknell University Press, 1980).
— *The Right Promethean Fire* (Urbana: University of Illinois Press, 1980).

Stephen W. Hawking, *A Brief History of Time* (New York: Bantam, 1988).

Douglas Hofstadter, *Gödel, Escher, Bach* (New York: Vintage, 1979).

William James, *The Will to Believe, and other Essays in Popular Philosophy,* in *The Works of William James* (Cambridge: Harvard University Press, 1979).

Charles Jencks: *What is Post-Modernism?* (New York: St. Martins Press, 1986, 1987).

William Jordan, ed., *Restoration and Management Notes* (Madison, Wisconsin) (periodical).

Immanuel Kant, *Kant's Critique of Aesthetic Judgement,* trans. J. C. Meredith (Oxford: Oxford University Press, 1911).
— *Critique of Practical Reason,* trans. L. W. Beck (Chicago: University of Chicago Press, 1949).

Melvin Konner, *The Tangled Wing: Biological Constraints on the Human Spirit* (New York: Holt, Rinehart & Winston, 1982).

Thomas Kuhn, *The Structure of Scientific Revolutions* (Chicago: University of Chicago Press, 1962).

Vladimir Lefebvre, "The Fundamental Structures of Human Reflexion," in *Journal of Social and Biological Structures,* 10, 1987.

Konrad Lorenz, *On Aggrssion* (New York: Harcourt Brace, 1966).

James Lovelock, *Gaia: a New Look at Life on Earth* (Oxford; Oxford University Press, 1979).

James Lovelock and Michael Allaby, *The Greening of Mars* (Ne York: Warner Books, 1984).

Jean-Francois Lyotard: *The Postmodern Condition: A Report on Knowledge,* trans. Geoff Bennington and Brian Massumi (Minneapolis: Univesity of Minnesota Press, 1985).

Benoit Mandelbrot, *The Fractal Geometry of Nature* (New York: Freeman, 1977).

Lynn Margulis and Dorion Sagan, *Microcosmos: Four Billion Years of Microbial Evolution From Our Microbial Ancestors* (New York: Summit, 1986).

David Marr, *Vision* (New York: Freeman, 1982).

Robert Pirsig, *Zen and the Art of Motorcycle Maintenance* (New York: Bantam, 1974).

Ilya Prigogine and Isabelle Stengers, *Order out of Chaos: Man's New Dialogue with Nature* (New York: Bantam, 1984).

Erwin Schroedinger, *Science and Humanism: Physics in Our Time* (Cambridge, England: Cambridge University Press, 1951).

Sorin Sonea and Maurice Panisset, *A New Bacteriology* (Boston: Jones & Bartlett, 1983).

Ingo Rentschler, Barbara Herzberger, David Epstein, eds., *Beauty and the Brain: Biological Aspects of Aesthetics* (Basel, Boston, Berlin: Birkhauser, 1988).

Thomas J. Scheff, "Microlinguistics: A Theory of Social Action," *Sociological Theory,* 4, 1, 1968.
—*Microsociology: Emotion, Discourse and Social Structure* (Chicago: University of Chicago Press, 1990).

J. William Schopf, ed., *Earth's Earliest Biosphere: Its Origin and Evolution* (Princeton: Princeton University Press, 1983).

George A. Seielstad, *At The Heart of the Web: The Inevitable Genesis of Intelligent Life* (New York: Harcourt Brace, 1989).

Lynda Sexson, *Ordinarily Sacred* (New York: Crossroad, 1982).

Roger Sperry, *Science and Moral Priority* (Oxford: Blackwell, 1983).

H. S. Thayer, "The Right to Believe: William James' Reinterpretation of the Function of Religious Belief," *Kenyon Review*, Winter, 1983.

Henry David Thoreau, *Walden* (Charles E. Merrill, Columbus, Ohio. 1969).

Frederick Turner, *A Double Shadow* (New York: Berkley, 1978).
—*Natural Classicism* (New York: Paragon House, 1985).
—*Genesis* (Dallas, San Francisco, New York: Saybrook Publishers, 1988).

Victor W. Turner, *Schism and Continuity in an African Society* (Manchester: Manchester University Press, 1957).
—*The Forest Of Symbols* (Ithaca: Cornell University Press, 1967).
—*The Drums of Affliction* (Oxford: Oxford University Press, 1968).
—*The Ritual Process* (Chicago: Aldine Pubs., 1969).
—*Dramas, Fields, and Metaphors* (Ithaca: Cornell University Press, 1974).
—*From Ritual to Theater* (New York: Performing Arts Journal Press, 1982).

John Varley, *Demon* (New York: Berkley, 1984).
—*The Persistence of Vision* (New York: Berkley, 1985).

Judith Wechsler, ed., *On Aesthetics in Science* (Cambridge, Mass.: M.I.T. Press, 1978).

Harvey Wheeler, ed., *The Journal of Social and Biological Structures* (Carpinteria, California) (periodical).

John Archibald Wheeler, "World as System Self-Synthesized by Quantum Networking," *IBM Journal of Research and Development*, Jan. 1988, vol. 32, no. 1.

Alfred North Whitehead, *Science and the Modern World* (Cambridge: Cambridge University Press, 1967).

Edward O. Wilson and Charles J. Lumsden, *Promethean Fire* (Cambridge: Harvard University Press, 1987).

Gene Wise, *American Historical Explanations* (Minneapolis: University of Minnesota Press, 1980).

Ludwig Wittgenstein, *Tractatus Logico-Philosophicus*, trans. C. K. Ogden (New York: Kegan Paul, 1933).

Virginia Woolf, *The Waves* (New York: Harcourt, Brace, 1931).
—*To the Lighthouse* (1927; New York: Harcourt Brace, 1955).
—*A Room of One's Own* (New York: Harcourt Brace, 1957).

E. C. Zeeman, "Catastrophe Theory," *Scientific American,* April, 1976.

INDEX